BASIC

ECONOMIC SECURITY FOR ALL CANADIANS

Basic Income

Economic Security for All Canadians

Sally Lerner

C.M.A. Clark

W.R. Needham

Between the Lines
Toronto

Basic Income

© 1999 by Sally Lerner, C.M.A. Clark, and W.R. Needham

First published in Canada in 1999 by
Between the Lines
720 Bathurst Street, Suite #404
Toronto, Ontario
M5S 2R4

Canadian Cataloguing in Publication Data

Lerner, Sally
   Basic income : economic security for all Canadians
Includes bibliographical references.
ISBN 1-896357-31-8
1. Guaranteed annual income—Canada.   I. Clark, Charles Michael
Andres.   II. Needham, W. Robert.   III. Title.

HC120.I5L47 1999   362.5'.82   C99-932053-X

Cover design and illustration by Lancaster Reid Creative
Interior design and page preparation by Steve Izma

Printed in Canada by University of Toronto Press

Between the Lines gratefully acknowledges assistance for its publishing activities from the Canada Council for the Arts, the Ontario Arts Council, and the Government of Canada through the Book Publishing Industry Development Program.

CONTENTS

ACKNOWLEDGEMENTS

My thanks go to the many people who have contributed to my understanding of the issues dealt with in this book, particularly James Robertson, Futurework colleague Arthur Cordell and BIEN stalwarts Philippe Van Parijs and Guy Standing. Ursula Franklin has supported my efforts as only she can do. George Francis holds the steady light.

— Sally Lerner

I would like to thank Sean Healy, Brigid Reynolds and Margaret John Kelly for constant inspiration.

— Charles M.A. Clark

There has been one person above all others who has kept me staying the course, as it were, in trying to elucidate an alternative social economics. That is the late Joan Robinson.

— W. Robert Needham

I come to two pieces of the unfinished business of the century and millennium that have high visibility and urgency. The first is the very large number of the very poor even in the richest of countries and notably in the U.S. . . . The answer or part of the answer is rather clear: Everybody should be guaranteed a decent basic income. A rich country . . . can well afford to keep everybody out of poverty.   — John Kenneth Galbraith, 1999

Let's Play a Mind Game about the Future of Work in Canada . . .

Imagine a time in the near future when full-time, secure, adequately waged jobs are even less available to many Canadians than they are now.

Most manufacturing and much knowledge and service work is done in developing countries or by Canadians who earn less than is required to participate fully in Canadian society—that is, to purchase adequate food, shelter, transportation, clothing, education and the basic amenities for themselves and their children. A majority of families would fall below the poverty line if one of their two earners became unemployed. And smart machines continue to displace people. High-tech jobs and highly skilled people still alternately chase one another, but this is a sector in which a substantial number cannot participate and which, in any case, has seen no explosion of employment demand.

The "flexible" workforce is a reality. Few private-sector organizations need more permanent full-time employees, and after outsourcing—spinning off as many tasks as possible to outside firms that compete fiercely for contracts—they have all the goods and service suppliers they can use, at far less cost. The public sector, once the employer of last resort, now operates more like the private sector. Its core functions, which are redefined frequently, are handled by lean staffs geared to continuous improvement of efficiency and maintenance of zero deficits. All other functions are outsourced. Temp agencies thrive, supplying "just-in-time" workers for most employers' needs.

Education and medical care, once considered basic public-sector responsibilities, rely more and more on private-sector partnerships and privatized delivery. Many other public goods and necessities, such as infrastructure maintenance, postal service and prison operation, are now supplied largely by private-sector firms that must attend to their bottom lines in order to survive. Downsizing continues. Our corporate and political leaders tell us "there is no alternative."

A user-pay philosophy prevails and many people cannot pay. Day care and education are funded only minimally; recreation, art and music programs for youth—together with libraries and museums—are seen as frills; environmental protection and remediation are not priorities for either the public or private sector; declining numbers of social workers cannot cope with increasing cases of malnutrition, substance abuse, mental illness, family breakdown, juvenile violence and other outcomes of unemployment, insecure employment and increasing disruption of family life. People who had once volunteered their time to fill such community needs are too hard-pressed themselves piecing together a living to continue volunteering for anything.

For the affluent 20 percent there is no big problem. They *can* pay for what they need and want, their children have the best of everything and gated communities are as available in Oakville as in Palm Beach.

If you aren't enjoying this mind game, that's good.
Because the Canada of the future can be very different.
We are not stuck with this scenario.
There are alternatives.
We do have choices.
This book is about some of these choices.

INTRODUCTION

*H*OW CAN AVERAGE CANADIANS best look after their interests in this era of new technologies and a globalizing economy? We must think carefully about the choices we make now, in view of these realities:

- Fewer Canadian workers without postsecondary education are needed to manufacture goods and provide services;
- Of the jobs that do exist, fewer are full-time, secure or adequately waged and more are part-time, temporary and contract positions, with inadequate pay levels, few if any benefits and no security;
- Postsecondary education is seen as nearly essential to earning a decent living, and is increasingly expensive;
- Wealth and incomes are polarizing as the rich get richer, middle-income ranks are reduced and insecure, and lower-income people face a shredded safety net and poor prospects for their children.

This book is centrally about why and how the establishment of an adequate Basic Income as a citizenship right of all Canadians can be an effective response to three major challenges currently facing Canada because of these new realities.

The first challenge is how to maintain full engagement of Canadians in their families, communities and the larger society if employment for all in secure, adequately waged jobs becomes an unrealistic goal.

Many people sincerely believe that the only path to a bright future for Canada lies in trying to return to a time of traditional full employment. They argue that the private sector will create jobs if more tax breaks and other incentives appear, that the public sector could become the employer of last resort, that a thirty-hour work week would spread existing employment around, that well-designed training can deliver workers with the skills that employers need, that a more entrepreneurial culture would spawn myriad small businesses to create countless new jobs.

Arguably, there is some truth in each of these claims. But there are also difficulties with each in terms of implementation, long-term effectiveness or political acceptability. Not least, none of them faces squarely the sea change in the world of work driven by the twin engines of radical technological change and rapid economic globalization. The essence of that change is that while wealth continues to be created, there is less need for people's labour in manufacturing and many services; when human labour is needed, increasingly it can be found in low-wage countries or structured to be low-wage at home—part-time, no benefits. The demand for a flexible workforce is the current code for this transformation, and governments are not cushioning the sea change (Yalnizyan 1998).

The second challenge Canadians face is how to plan effectively for the better quality of life that the new economic and technological realities can offer if these fundamental changes are steered in positive directions. Basic Income—ideally a sufficient amount to live decently provided to every Canadian citizen—is envisoned not simply as a cheque in the mail but as the keystone of basic economic security, embedded in a social context that assures universal access to decent housing, health care and education as well as varied opportunities to contribute to community, social and material well-being.

With the establishment of all citizens' access to basic economic security, social consensus would develop over time about the individual's responsibility to engage in needed activities for the community, the environment and the general social good. We could educate our children differently, with more emphasis on creativity and cooperation, less on competing and following orders. People would, of course, still seek paid employment for additional income, or even do a Bill Gates. And most people would want paid employment, for social contacts and intellectual stimulation as well as for the income. But no stigma would attach to those who lived on the Basic Income and devoted their time to unpaid activities.

The flexible workforce so desired by employers could become a reality because workers would be on secure financial ground as they moved among temporary jobs and contracts: "flexecurity" is what it's called in Europe (Huws 1997). There would be more real freedom and life choices for Canadians—a rightful harvest from the new wealth created by the much-heralded information age. As one of the world's richest countries, Canada can afford to take leadership in modelling ways to provide a better quality of life by steering fundamental change in positive directions.

The third challenge we must respond to is the necessity of caring for the environment, of maintaining ourselves in ways that are less destructive of our childrens' future. This also means that we must change how we work and distribute income: sheer growth based on energy use and throughput of materials is arguably not an option, particularly if proposed as a model for the developing world as well. To keep mining dirty coal so that workers can continue to earn a wage by going into the mines simply doesn't make sense, for the workers or for the environment.

It is clear to an increasing number of thoughtful analysts that new ways of working can open paths to more satisfying family and community life. It is also clear that there may be some extremely negative outcomes globally if those with power and wealth refuse to act in their own best interests by distributing resources so that individual dignity, community stability and a sound consumer base are renewed and preserved. How to do this sustainably should become the subject of informed public discussion among Canadians.

This book is intended to stimulate discussion of a Basic Income (BI) for all Canadians as a realistic policy choice to ensure positive outcomes from the continuing global societal transformation:

- Chapter 1 explores the new realities we must deal with.
- Chapter 2 examines the concept of BI and the issues it raises.
- Chapter 3 provides a brief history of the BI idea in Canada.
- Chapter 4 overviews the need and rationale for a Canadian BI, and details its benefits.
- Chapter 5 looks at an example of a BI for Canada.

Let's play a new mind game . . . looks at a future that works for Canada.

A Basic Income discussion guide and five articles for additional reading conclude the book.

1

New Realities and the Need for Basic Economic Security

> We need to see that the welfare state must be rebuilt so that the risks of fragile work are socialised rather than being borne increasingly by the individual. We must, in short, turn the new precarious forms of employment into a right to discontinuous waged work and a right to disposable time. It must be made possible for every human being autonomously to shape his or her life and create a balance between family, paid employment, leisure and political commitment. And I truly believe that this is the only way of forming a policy that will create more employment for everybody.
>
> — Ulrich Beck, "Goodbye to All That Wage Slavery"

THERE IS MOUNTING EVIDENCE that ensuring basic economic security for all Canadians must become a top-level political priority. The continuing fundamental changes in the nature of work resulting from globalization and rapid technological advances are well-documented in contemporary literature.[1] Consequently, this book's focus is on the examination and advocacy of a Canadian Basic Income to serve as the foundation of that economic security. Far from being a Luddite tract, it suggests that technological breakthroughs open the door to a more human way of life, to a world where people will less and less have to perform machine-like tasks, and will be far freer to find fulfillment in family, community and creative endeavours—if we can get the economics right.

Basic Income (BI) has been proposed a number of times under a variety of names in different countries. Its core aim is to make sure that all citizens have an income that enables them to live decently and participate fully in the economy and community life. This chapter provides an overview of the ongoing societal transformation and an introduction to BI as a feasible and desirable response.

Numerous versions of BI programs have been considered over the past half century and the idea is being viewed with interest once again. Reflecting on various scenarios for Canada's next decade, a respected Ottawa policy analyst suggests the possibility that shrinking numbers of paid jobs due to technological change may mean that "by 2005, a GAI or Guaranteed Annual Income will emerge, combining Employment Insurance, social assistance, seniors' pensions, child allowances, etc. into one system of payment" (McCracken 1997:12).

A long-time European advocate of BI sums up our current dilemma this way:

> As long as most wage earners contribute to the production of wealth, the problem of distributing wealth is solved by each individual's employment contract and the family support and social security arrangements tied to it. Once this ceases to be the case and this supposedly "normal" condition . . . has disappeared for good, the problem of distribution can be solved only by establishing specific economic rights that all citizens grant each other as a component of their citizenship. The central idea of a "citizens' [basic] income" consists in the right to sufficient income not conditional upon gainful employment. (Offe 1996:129)

Addressing the question of how to reconcile economic flexibility (part-time and temporary jobs, contract work, movable workers, two-tier wage structures and the like) with social cohesion, a 1996 OECD Forum on the Future concluded that "the introduction of a universal citizen's income intended to put greater value on the broad range of human activities that extends well beyond paid work" is well worth considering (OECD 1997)

This book examines the arguments for and against BI, and details one model of how such a program might be financed and delivered in Canada. The contention is that Canadians should now begin to find ways to de-couple basic economic security from the traditional jobs that may not be there for a growing number of people. As a society, we must be prepared with the plans and means to sustain individual dignity, family well-being and community stability if the private sector has diminishing need for human labour.

The New Realities: A Closer Look

Economic globalization and technological change are irrevocably reshaping the nature of work: we are in the throes of a post-industrial revolution, or what some call a post-Fordist revolution as the assembly line gives way to the workerless production pod. That's good—so far. It frees people from the machine, but not from the economy. While some new types of jobs are emerging, developed societies such as Canada must no longer perpetuate the myth that secure, adequately waged employment is available for all. The effect of this myth is to manufacture consent for deserting and stigmatizing those most in need, and to dangerously postpone the effective societal action needed to steer global change in positive directions for Canada.

In the present context of jobless growth due to technological innovation and economic globalization, it is the increasing polarization of developed societies—into a marginalized, redundant, deskilled large minority and a small, affluent technical-professional elite—that must be faced and squarely dealt with by decision makers. Who's in the middle? The increasingly "anxious class" flagged by former U.S Labor Secretary Robert Reich in *The Work of Nations* (1992).

Without decisive and innovative action, this downward spiral, together with long-term un- and underemployment for increasing numbers of individuals and families, will exact an even heavier toll than at present. It will be felt in reduced purchasing power and material standard of living, as well as in eroded self-esteem, family breakdown, rising crime rates and all of the other well-documented consequences of unemployment and downward mobility. And the opportunities for a more human society based on technological innovation will remain unrealized.

To be sustainable over the long term, a society must ensure that all of its members have the basic resources to participate fully in that society. After the end of World War II, Canada set off boldly to reach that goal and, to a notable extent, succeeded. But by the end of the 1990s, Canadians seemed caught in a backward-running tide. In the wake of spending cuts that, in a number of provinces, swept supports from under those most in need of them—the unemployed and the growing ranks of the underemployed—most Canadians were fearful that irreparable damage was being done to their valued compassionate society. Hardest to swallow has been the blame laid on the victims. Most to be feared and fought is the assertion by those in power that there are no alternatives. There are other choices, and to prosper as a society, Canada must make them rather than succumb to the "cult of impotence" espoused by corporate and political naysayers (McQuaig 1998; Dobell 1996).

Our "Great Transformation"

As our elites push us firmly down the path of transformation from a labour-intensive manufacturing and resource-based society to one whose prosperity and global competitiveness will, we are told, depend on the ability to create and use information productively, revisiting history can be illuminating. Karl Polanyi's influential 1944 book, *The Great Transformation*, offers a clear account of people caught in the turmoil of the ascendence of the market economy, in what we now call the Industrial Revolution. It owes its contemporary influence to the relevance for our own great transformation of Polanyi's insights into the ideological conflicts and human suffering occasioned in eighteenth-century England by the transition from a rural agricultural and craft society to an industrialized urbanizing one.

Polanyi's main point is that as the Industrial Revolution gathered steam, the drive for a completely self-regulating market system free of any government interference would have led to disastrous consequences for workers and the environment (and eventually all of England) if there had not developed countervailing pressures for intervention to aid those who were left landless and destitute, with no means of creating a livelihood. The parallels to the current world situation of rapid economic globalization and technological change are striking and, one hopes, instructive. It is neither morally acceptable nor politically possible to build a sustainable new world order on the ruined lives of multitudes who can find no real place in it.

The history of public policy on unemployment reveals that the concept of unemployment developed erratically during and after the Industrial Revolution, veering between two views: that individuals without work were idle by choice and should be dealt with punitively, and a recognition that lack of paid employment or of a living wage for substantial numbers of people is a social problem to be addressed through labour exchanges, unemployment insurance, income supports, whatever means are required (Garraty 1978).

It is interesting to note the extent to which contemporary establishment musings on "welfare bums" and the need for workfare reproduce two-hundred-year-old concerns about idleness and solutions such as the workhouse. Perhaps the current reluctance of Canadian politicians to speak publicly about a future of work that may hold fewer adequate employment opportunities for increasing numbers of people stems from the fact that they currently have no innovative policies to deal with such a radical development.

Economic Insecurity as a Way of Life?

In Canada, thousands of manufacturing jobs have been permanently lost during the past decade. Currently, large chunks of service-sector employment, high-skilled and less-skilled alike, are in the process of being sent offshore, relegated to low-paying back-office operations or taken over by smart machines. Too much of the employment that remains or is created tends to be part-time, temporary, low-paid work—or reported as self-employment by people trying to generate income by some means or other. While about two-thirds of part-time workers choose to be part time, we don't know how many temporary and contract workers like their situation, and we can be certain that people who work full time or more for less than a living wage would prefer otherwise (Swift 1995; Campbell and others 1999).

We are told that there is no alternative to fundamental changes in the nature of work if Canadian companies are to compete successfully in the global market, and that the new information technologies will inevitably produce more good jobs, soon. But more and more "Canadian companies" (often U.S. branch plants to begin with) are multinational corporations with few ties to any one country and no legal or felt obligation to create jobs of any kind, good or bad, for Canadians. In the words of one influential study:

> The most disturbing aspect of this system is that the formidable power and mobility of global corporations are undermining the effectiveness of national governments to carry out essential policies on behalf of their people. Leaders of nation states are losing much of the control over their own territory that they once had. . . . Business enterprises that routinely operate across borders are linking far-flung pieces of territory into a new world economy that bypasses all sorts of established political arrangements and conventions. Tax laws intended for another age, traditional ways to control capital flows and interest rates, full-employment policies, and old approaches to resource development and environmental protection are becoming obsolete, unenforceable or irrelevant. (Barnet and Cavanagh 1994: 19)

But the multinational corporations are not completely free agents either. Another analyst puts it this way:

> As our economic system has detached from place and gained greater dominance over our democratic institutions, even the world's most powerful corporations have become captives of the forces of a globalized financial system that has delinked the creation of money from the creation of real wealth. . . . The big winners are the corporate raiders

who strip sound companies of their assets for short-term gain and the [financial] speculators. (Korten 1995: 12)

In short, corporations' major shareholders demand the highest short-term gain from their investments and insist that this be the sole priority of the corporate world. Corporations that resist, hoping perhaps to avoid laying off local workers, are quickly disciplined by global financial forces in much the same way that governments face the dictates of the major bond-rating organizations. It's that old golden rule again, on a global scale: those who have the gold make the rules. While not everyone agrees that globalization is so total and overwhelming that national governments have become irrelevant and unable to protect their citizens, this argument continues to make the rounds in company with the neo-conservative mantra that less government is best anyway (Hirst and Thompson 1996). So what's really going on? Most of us are unable to find any answers in the back of the book.

As a result of these global developments, Canadians face a growing "individualization of risk [as they] have had to shoulder more and more of the responsibility for adjusting to high unemployment, downsizing, industrial restructuring, and related trends" (Betcherman and Lowe 1997). Far from being able to come to grips with the transformation of their choices and chances, many Canadians are frozen in the onrushing headlights by anxiety about jobs, the economy and their inability to control the impacts of change on their lives. The prospect of being jobless, or so underemployed that we cannot establish families or provide for them, drives this sense of anxiety (Taylor 1998).

These fears now seem to pervade much of the middle class, eroding consumer confidence and feeding on the sense that our elected governments are running out on their responsibilities to steer and cushion this transition. Rather than seeking creative strategies and investing in people, governments seem to have put deficit reduction—certainly one important priority—ahead of everything else. The resulting budget-cutting binge, only now winding down, undermined and dangerously weakened the foundations of our society—the health care system, access to quality education and social support programs that Canadians depend on for their own well-being and that of their neighbours, especially in turbulent times. Was this the only alternative? Some think not (Torjman and Battle 1999).

How can we cope with the new rules of the new global game? Is it the only game in the world now, or can we take back more control of our work, our lives and our communities? We must begin to find a variety of innovative answers to these questions. We must begin to show the way for our governments to act.

Finding Positive Responses

Justice dictates that we not continue to penalize people who cannot find secure, living-wage jobs, but rather that we examine a range of other mechanisms for allocating work and distributing income. These might include work-time reduction—through a shorter work week, job sharing, discouraging overtime, earlier retirement and innovative mixes of these ideas in conjunction with sabbatical leaves based on some form of time-bank that would allow individuals to accumulate waged time. But work-time reduction can be viewed as only one component in a strategy to adapt to growing structural un- and underemployment. And no strategy is likely to be successful in equitably addressing the new problems of income distribution without the introduction of some form of adequate and secure BI—to meet basic needs and to serve as the foundation, the *base* on which we can build our livelihoods.

Certainly there have been telling arguments in favour of progressive versions of BI. One is the need to adequately compensate work vital to the well-being of communities, such as child and elder care. Another is the necessity of maintaining consumer spending power, an obvious and practical point. A fundamental argument is that productivity and prosperity in the private sector have been made possible not only by much unpaid work but, crucially, by social investment (taxpayers' money) over time in health, education, law and order, research and development and infrastructure: the necessary foundation of a stable, productive society. In this view, a secure BI is a just means to underpin the peaceful transition to a new era of less traditional employment, with its possibility of richer, more varied lives for all Canadians.

A powerful and long-lived BI rationale, one with which many people are acutely uncomfortable, is this: because the earth, its land and resources, is the common heritage of all people, everyone has a right to a share in this heritage in the form of a BI financed from rents paid by those who have appropriated the use of land and resources. Putting aside concerns about how this idea might be labelled, one can certainly argue that, just as corporations were initially required to show evidence that they contributed in some way to the public good, so all landholders and resource users should now and in future be required either to provide adequately waged employment to all or contribute substantially to funding some form of BI. The increasing polarization between rich and poor, within the developed nations as well as between North and South, is clear evidence that both pragmatic and justice-based arguments for the provision of basic economic security are being conveniently ignored.

A Canadian BI could be financed in a variety of ways: by discontinuing billions in subsidies to corporations, closing down most welfare bureaucracies and levying an earmarked value-added tax (VAT) on nonessential goods and services, or at least on "the goods and services of the high technology revolution" (Rifkin 1995). A very small Tobin tax on financial speculation (ul Haq and others 1996) or a minuscule "bit tax" on all electronic transactions (Cordell and Ide 1997) are other feasible components of BI financing strategies if broad support for them were forthcoming from the other OECD countries. Chapter 5 provides a model of one financing option.

As citizens of a national state that supports the idea of democratically elected, accountable federal and provincial governments, we need to discuss what messages we want to deliver to our politicians in the next crucial years. How we work and the stability of our livelihoods are changing fundamentally. We need positive responses to these changes from governments and the private sector. This may be the right time to demand that our elected decision makers establish basic economic security as a right for all Canadians and social responsibility as an obligation of all corporations.

2

WHAT IS BASIC INCOME?

[Basic Income could provide] the benefits which the traditional upper-middle classes derived from the possession of a modest private income which gave them a degree of independence and saved them from being complete wage slaves. European civilization, as it developed from the Renaissance onwards, depended on unearned income and inherited wealth. Among the nineteenth- and early twentieth-century European bourgeoisie, a private income was for long a supplement to income from work—and a major element of flexibility. It enabled people to embark on careers which would not otherwise be possible and to take risks with their professions and life styles. . . . But the lip service paid to the work ethic leads to silence on these matters. In fact, the main thing wrong with unearned income is that too few of us have it.

— Samuel Brittan, *Capitalism with a Human Face*

THE FOCUS OF THIS BOOK'S EXAMINATION of the BI concept is the Basic Income European Network (BIEN) definition of BI as *an income unconditionally granted to all citizens on an individual basis.*[1]

The influential book *Basic Income: Freedom from Poverty, Freedom to Work* by British BI advocate Tony Walter elaborates this definition as follows:

Basic income would be paid to each man, woman and child, as individuals; payment would not be conditional on other income or lack of it, nor on willingness to work, nor on gender. It would be paid to all those currently domiciled in a country. The level of basic income would vary by age, replacing pensions and child allowances, with supplements for those without other income or who incur extra living costs [e.g., through illness or other disability]. This system would replace social security and welfare payments, and personal allowances and tax reliefs as far as is practical. Income tax would be paid from the first pound, dollar, franc or mark of extra income, but the basic income itself would not be taxable. Separate national insurance or social security funds would be abolished. The unit for both basic income and income tax would be the individual rather than the nuclear family.

For those earning, or with unearned income, the individual's net income would be Basic Income plus Other Income minus Income Tax on Other Income. In practice, the basic income would be deducted from the tax due, as a tax credit. For individuals without other income, basic income would be paid by monthly or weekly cheque. For part-time workers paying less income tax than the value of their basic income, the excess of basic income over tax could either be paid as a supplement in the wage packet, or by separate cheque. For children, basic income could be paid direct to the parent who cares for the child. (Walter 1989: 18)

Interestingly, Walter prefaced his book with a warning to the reader not to fall into the typical traps of seeing BI as (1) completely unthinkable because it would encourage free riding and social disintegration, (2) the instant solution to all societal problems, or (3) a fine idea for a distant utopian future (1989: 8). In this book we hope to help our readers avoid those traps by presenting BI as a policy proposal now worth considering for Canada, but not without its contentious aspects.

A variety of similar ideas about basic economic security have been considered and proposed under different names—Negative Income Tax (NIT), Guaranteed Annual Income (GAI), Citizen's Income (CI), Social Wage, Social Dividend. Some Canadian versions are described in chapter 3. These differ from BI in some basic premises as well as in numerous details, and being aware of them is useful in understanding the questions about BI that need widespread discussion if we are to arrive at some consensus about why and how we want to ensure basic economic security for all Canadians.

The most controversial questions raised about BI and similar proposals are:

- Who should receive a BI? (chap. 2)
- What conditions, if any, should be attached to receiving a BI? (chap. 2)
- What would be the positive effects of a BI (chap. 4)
- What should be the amount of a BI and how should it be introduced? (chap. 5)

- How would a BI be financed? (chap. 5)

Let's look at the first two questions.

Who Should Receive a Basic Income?

Should a BI be universal—that is, go to everyone—or should there be targeted (means-tested) income support only for the poor (the working poor, the deserving poor, all poor), only for the unemployed, or only for certain age groups? There are also certain to be other questions, such as whether BI should go to families or to every individual and when immigrants would be eligible for BI.

Even though universal entitlement programs such as the Canada Pension Plan and the Family Allowance have been accepted in Canada, the universality question remains fundamentally controversial. Many people feel strongly that financial support should go only to those who provide means-tested evidence that they really need it, and that it would be a waste of money to give everyone a BI.

So we need to examine the arguments for and against a universal BI compared with targeted income support such as we have now. A recent analysis (Boston and others 1998), drawing on New Zealand's experience with tighter targeting of social assistance, makes these points:

- Targeting aid to the poor is promoted as the cheapest and most cost-effective way of eliminating poverty and providing a minimum standard of living for all. But if a targeted program encourages strategies to conceal extra income (because it deducts any earned income dollar for dollar from social support payments—the poverty trap so common to targeted programs), some of these savings are lost.
- Over the long term, means-tested programs may save money only because cutting benefits to the poor is more politically acceptable than trimming aid that goes to all or most of the population. If single mothers on welfare receive less than they need to live on and feed their children, this may cut costs but defeat the purpose of the aid.
- Opponents of universality argue that it allows too much "middle-class capture" of benefits, thereby reducing its effectiveness in closing the rich-poor gap, and that targeting remedies this. But the multiple objectives of modern social support systems go beyond greater vertical equity to goals of "promotion of social cohesion and racial tolerance, and minimizing of social differentiation and stratification" that universalism addresses.

- For many advocates, the economic and moral justifications for a universal BI turn largely on the fact that it avoids the many problems associated with targeted programs: they are difficult and costly to administer (high transaction costs), inefficient, inequitable, intrusive, stigmatize the poor and undermine middle-class support for social programs and income.
- More positively, a universal BI would bolster political support for maintaining BI at a level that would enable people to live decently if paid work were scarce or did not pay a living wage. Universal benefits have proven to be politically more cut-resistant than those targeted to the most vulnerable in society, not least because the middle class has the skills to lobby effectively in its own interest.

The real challenge, it seems, is to gain public acceptance of a universal BI in the first place. Attempting to sort out the controversy, the New Zealand researchers compared targeted with universal programs, concluding that:

> any evaluation of the relative merits of targeting versus universality depends in large measure on what one is seeking to achieve. . . . If the aims of social assistance are broad and multiple—as has been the case in most OECD countries—then it is by no means self-evident that targeting is always the best or most efficient option.
>
> Generally speaking, the greater the weight given to fostering social cohesion and building a just society (in all its multifarious dimensions—including equity between social classes, races and different age groups, equity between and within families, equitable access to education and health care, and so on), the stronger the case for universalism. . . . Such objectives necessitate a heavy reliance on universal assistance. (Boston and others 1998)

What about Conditionality?

Should a Canadian BI be unconditional, a right of citizenship, or should it require some type of socially useful work—or just plain work of any kind—in return for receiving it? This question, perhaps even more than that of universality, provokes strong responses. Primarily, negative reactions against an unconditional BI come from those who reject anything that smacks of "something for nothing," resent free riders, and fear a deterioration of multitudes of people into couch potatoes or worse.

An unconditional BI is often perceived as giving something for nothing to people who are not in paid work and seems to many simply unfair to those who are employed and pay taxes. There is an assumption, fostered in recent years by the mainstream media, that anyone not totally incapable of working who *really wants* a job can get one—or two if need be—that will provide an adequate living. So when people turn to welfare they are portrayed as looking for a handout, and the prescription is some form of workfare—wash dishes for your free meal—usually lauded for its value in making people more employable.

Yet workfare—forcing people to work (or in some cases to train)—has many problems, including lack of suitable jobs, downgrading of volunteer activities, exposing welfare recipients to exploitation, pushing employed people out of jobs and engendering hopes for post-training employment that may not materialize. The few workfare success stories that make the news hide the embarrassing facts that workfare cannot create real jobs for all and is vulnerable to criticism as a violation of human rights. Fair workfare that would provide child care and job training that leads to living-wage jobs is still only an expensive dream (Solow 1998).

New Views of Reciprocity and Equity

Conditionality is really about the question of reciprocity—the ethical principle of mutual giving and receiving—and about equity. These concerns centrally influence how people respond to the idea of an unconditional BI. They deserve careful consideration because Canadians will want to think about some graduated alternatives between a completely unconditional BI and tightly enforced workfare in considering how a BI might work. A few interesting models are already in place. In Ireland, for example, communities create useful jobs that pay at the going rate and can be voluntarily taken up by the unemployed as an alternative to welfare.

A recent analysis of reciprocity (Widerquist 1998) makes some interesting arguments in favour of an unconditional BI:

- Forcing people to work or seek work in return for welfare or a BI violates the reciprocity principle of "(S)he who does not work, will not eat" because the requirement is not applied to owners of land, natural resource rights, capital, government bonds or other assets that permit them to have an income without working. An unconditional BI eliminates this violation of reciprocity since citizens work and participate in the economy by choice—no one is more or less coerced than others.
- With respect to equity, defined as an envy-free situation, BI offers citizens two choices:

[D]o not work and receive the unconditional income or work and receive a higher income. Reciprocity exists in the sense that all people are equal before the law: the same rules apply to everyone. People have the right to choose to work or not to work. Those who choose to work must, therefore, find it preferable to not working. Revealed preference shows that they do not envy those who choose not to work, because if they did they would choose not to work. . . . The same [no cause for envy] cannot be said for someone who lives off the basic income. . . . There could be any number of reasons why a person living off of a basic income might want—but be unable—to trade places with someone who works. . . . If one defines inequity as having privileges that are not available to anyone else, one can say a person living purely off of an unconditional income might be in an inequitable position compared to a worker, but one cannot say that a worker is in an inequitable position compared to those who live off an unconditional income. Therefore, based on the principle of reciprocity, one cannot say that the existence of a Guaranteed Income exploits workers to benefit nonworkers. (Widerquist 1998: 5-6)

Earning—But Not a Living

That there is an active "living wage" movement in the U.S. points to the fact that workers there are increasingly forced to take inadequately waged jobs that often offer little or nothing in the way of income security, much less benefits or safety and health protection (Pollin and Luce 1998). Canada's proportion of low-paying jobs is second only to that of the U.S. among OECD countries. Among full-time Canadian workers in 1996, 16 percent of men and 34 percent of women were low paid (that is, had wages less than two-thirds of median earnings among full-time employees). Nearly 12 percent of Canadians working full time in 1996 earned less than $15,000; for women, the figure was 16 percent (Yalnizyan 1998: 22).

In Canada,

between 1981 and 1996 the earned income of the poorest 20 percent of households with dependent children was cut in half, from an average of $12,000 (1996 dollars) to $6,000. Government help (unemployment insurance, social assistance and other programs) brought the poor family's after-tax income up to $16,600. This is lower than it was in 1980 ($17,700 in 1996 dollars). This government support, crucial to maintaining social cohesion in Canada during any slide in employment and wage levels, has eroded over the past 15 years and particularly since 1995. Both the working and non-working poor have been left with fewer personal resources and less protection from "rent-poverty." (Yalnizyan 1998: 53-56)

A BI set at a decent-living level would afford lower-income people the choice of turning down inadequately waged jobs, which would cause wages to rise, particularly for unpleasant jobs. While this might be offset to some extent by people willing to work for less at jobs they enjoy or happy to top up the BI with part-time, low-demand work, the overall outcome would be more choice and more work for the marginally in-demand. Forcing the poor into the labour market without a BI program or even an adequate minimum wage puts them in a prime position to be exploited and violates the principle of reciprocity, since those with independent assets are not forced into this position (Widerquist 1998.)

Proposing a BI at a decent-living level always raises the issue of work incentives: will many people opt to work less or not at all? It's important to remember that a BI would allow for virtually no luxuries and that a person who engaged in paid work would always be better off because poverty/employment traps wouldn't exist—the paid worker would keep the full amount of the BI, paying taxes only on anything earned over that amount. But is there any evidence to support the claim that workers want to work even when provided with income supports?

Everyday observations suggest that the victims of plant layoffs continue to want to work. They have not chosen to be unemployed. A scan of the daily newspaper documents the large number of citizens who are willing to work and who regularly turn out to apply for small numbers of job openings when, and indeed even before, new job openings are officially announced.

Consistent with these observations, empirical studies undertaken in Canada and the United States suggest that the desire for a job is not significantly weakened by income maintenance and the tax-cash transfer system that is used to support incomes at more adequate levels. A study of data from the Manitoba Mincome Experiment and from related U.S. studies[2] concluded that: "individuals and families are likely to be fairly insensitive to changes in the tax-transfer system facing them."[3] In other words, they do not need incentives to work, and the incentive to work is not affected by social provision.

Further, a Canadian study published in March 1998 reported that individuals in a test program receiving Canadian Income Assistance (IA) "were reluctant to remain on IA longer just to gain eligibility for . . . a generous earnings supplement made available to those who find full-time jobs . . . because they disliked welfare and because it was difficult to find work." The earnings supplement would have been made available to eligible applicants in British Columbia and New Brunswick under what was called SSP (Self-Sufficiency Project).

The SSP report suggested that "working poor people . . . would be unlikely to enter the welfare rolls and wait the required year [on IA] just to [in this way] qualify for an [SSP] earnings supplement" and that "concerns about entry effects [into new social programs as opposed to work] may be somewhat overstated."[4] This also implies that income support programs and a guaranteed annual income would not destroy the incentive to work.

The SSP study also provided anecdotal accounts of the voices of the unemployed who were taking part in the study. Generally their stories, are consistent with people wanting to work and not needing any incentive to do so. For example: "I did temp work in between interviews; I scoured the papers. . . . Everyday was a workday trying to find a job."[5]

The evidence from unemployment statistics, statistical analysis and anecdotal accounts is consistent in indicating that people want to work (Solow 1998). It is *income-yielding work that is wanting, not people's motivation*. Those who argue that supplements to earned incomes destroy work incentives are in effect, whether intentionally or unintentionally, shifting the responsibility for unemployment, poverty and their related effects from the operations of businesses and governments to the individual victims of the joint policies of business and governments. Empirical evidence and anecdotal accounts all suggest that BI has logic on its side. Blaming the victims is not an option.

BI: A New Path in a New Economy —Reason in the economy

Andre Gorz (1997, 1985), a well-known French social analyst and BI advocate, supports a BI that is adequate to live on. He argues for an unconditional BI because:

- A "conditional" BI would be "inconsistent with the perspectives opened and changes effected by post-fordism": that is, the shift to a service economy that makes it difficult to quantify and measure labour;
- As a basic livelihood for all that can be topped up by labour income, BI will be the best lever to redistribute as widely as possible both paid and unpaid activities;
- Unconditionality preserves the uncoerced nature of voluntary activities (art, culture, family, mutual aid and the like) "which only have their full meaning if they are accomplished for their own sake";
- An unconditional basic income is best adapted to an economy in

which knowledge has become the main productive force. It "turns the right to the development of one's capacities into an unconditional right to an autonomy which transcends its productive functions"; that is, an unconditional BI allows at least partial de-commodification of people, their selves and their abilities;

- An unconditional BI is best suited to use the wealth collectively produced in order to free people's time and to eliminate paid work as the dominant form of human activity.

Gorz sees an unconditional BI as an activity multiplier rather than an activity reducer, "not as an exemption from doing anything but, on the contrary, as the possibility for all to unfold thousands of activities, individual and collective, private and public, which can now develop without needing to be profitable." He notes, as we do, that the transformation to such a positive BI society would require numerous changes in addition to the BI. Gorz flags the need for promotion of local economic trading systems (LETS) and appropriate town planning (*Basic Income* 28: 140-51).

In thinking about conditionality, it also seems clear that changing how we educate children and what we reward in our societies will gradually produce citizens who take for granted that they will blend paid work, community service, parenting and self-development into a richer way of life. Indeed, enforced idleness would be seen as cruel and unusual punishment.

Needed: A New Canadian Dialogue

Basic Income is not a new idea in Canada. It has been promoted from both ends of the political spectrum. Recently, the idea of an *adequate* BI has gathered support from a variety of groups, both grassroots activists and academics, who see the world of work changing radically toward a future of jobless growth or, less dramatically, of insecure contingent employment for the growing ranks of just-in-time workers who will make up the flexible workforce (Chancer 1998; Pollin and Luce 1998). On the other hand, those who want to scale back the welfare state and ensure a strong "work incentive" like the idea of collapsing virtually all state support programs and providing a very *minimal* BI. The Macdonald Commission in 1985 took this approach, favouring a guaranteed annual income of $2,750 per adult and $750 per child (Yalnizyan 1998: 102). More about this in chapter 3.

Opposition to the idea of a BI has also come in several flavours. Many people raised to revere the work ethic fear that a BI, if set at a level to permit a decent life, would reward idleness and create legions of free riders. Others, particularly in the labour movement and anti-poverty groups, fear the creation of a Macdonald Commission-style BI so inadequate that it would benefit only employers and promote a race to the bottom in terms of wages and workplace standards as people in below-subsistence poverty competed fiercely for diminishing hours of paid work.

It is clear that the idea of a BI raises many contentious issues. Universality and unconditionality need a great deal of public discussion in Canada if we are to move beyond instant negative reactions on the part of many people. Despite Canadians' support for universal entitlement programs, there are powerful traditions and ideologies behind the dictum that limited resources should be targeted only to those who can prove they need help and are looking for paid work. Willingness on the part of Canadians to question this conventional thinking, particularly in terms of what we should value as work, must be at the heart of any consideration of a BI for Canada.

On the basis of this overview, it is tempting to suggest that the question "What is Basic Income?" should really be "How can we design an adequate and politically acceptable BI for Canada?" Before tackling that challenge, though, let's look in more detail at the policy context for a BI in Canada.

3

Basic Income in the Canadian Policy Context

Study Paints Bleak Job Scene in Canada
Jobless figures don't measure underemployment, report
contends (June 3, 1999)
Canadian workers are underpaid and underemployed,
says a report released yesterday by Ryerson Polytechnic
University. The study, conducted by the Ryerson Social
Reporting Network, observes that 52% of Canadians are
paid less than $15 an hour, and that 45% of the country's
workforce is engaged in "flexible" work, with people
unable to find full-time or permanent jobs. . . . The
Ryerson study estimates that as many as 20.3% of
Canadians are underemployed or otherwise lack
employment security and an adequate level of wages.
— James Cudmore, *The National Post*

The Social Policy Context since the 1930s

PRIOR TO THE GREAT DEPRESSION of the 1930s, Canadians who had no
employment or other means of support had to depend on "local and
voluntary sources of relief (and 'make-work' projects) such as mutual
aid circles, religious and civic associations, extended families,
immigrant ghettos and neighbours; and in urban centres, 'indoor relief'
in the form of workhouses and prisons" (Yalnizyan and others 1994:
30-31). During the 1930s, widespread hardship led to protest
movements such as the aborted 1935 "On to Ottawa" trek, in which
thousands of Western Canadians demanded employment other than
that provided by the coercive work camps of the period.

Such actions had their impact. As early as 1937, the federal
government was emphasizing the need for "collective efforts to
promote economic development and collective assumption of the

24

responsibility for the alleviation of individual distress." The Rowell-Sirois Commission stressed that "rising standards of public welfare and education had come to play an immensely important part in the economic affairs of the country."[1] This perspective eventually consolidated the rights of respective governments to their "fair" share of national resources in order to discharge their responsibilities to "a) promot[e] equal opportunities for the well-being of all Canadians; b) [further] economic development to reduce disparity in opportunity; c) provid[e] essential public services of reasonable quality to all Canadians" (Constitution Act, 1982, s. 36).

Building from the initiatives in the Depression years, and with a new sense of nationhood and common cause that grew out of involvement in World War II, Canadians developed

> a relatively broad social consensus from the end of the 1930s to the beginning of the 1970s . . . [and an] evocative new language of citizenship, a language of rights to the provision of certain protections and access to services. The expansion of individual rights was couched in two powerful concepts: one of *uniform protection across the country*, essentially giving concrete form to national citizenship; and the growing notion of *universality* of certain minimums, albeit basic and categorical, "obtainable as of right and in the company of all other citizens." (Yalnizan and others 1994: 33)

One assumption that underlay the construction of the Canadian welfare state was that there would be full employment—jobs for all who wanted to work, and thus a firm financial basis for the foundation programs: Old Age Security (1927), Unemployment Insurance (1940), Family Allowance 1945), the formalization of equalization payments (1957), the Canada Pension Plan (1964), the Canada Assistance Plan (1966) and Medicare (1966). Other necessary conditions for the functioning of the Canadian welfare state were the availability of capital for investment within the country and a low interest-rate policy.

In the late 1950s rising unemployment rates and technological innovation created a more turbulent job market in Canada, and the 1960s brought strong pressures to "solve" problems of poverty. In 1968, the Senate Committee on Poverty was created to "investigate all aspects of poverty and recommend effective policy measures. When its findings were presented in 1971 (the Croll Report), it recommended that [existing] programs be scrapped and replaced by a guaranteeed annual income scheme" (Yalnizyan and others 1994: 35). This plan took a negative income tax approach and proposed a guaranteed income of 70 percent of poverty lines established by the Committee, with a 70 percent tax-back rate on additional income. The plan was never implemented. Instead, a new Social Security Review was established in 1973.

From 1973 to 1976 Lalonde's Social Security Review struggled once again with formulas for defeating poverty. But it was widely seen as a failure—"noodling with the tax system and revenue neutral programs of income supplementation (e.g., refundable child tax credits) had replaced any notion of guaranteeing a social minimum for citizens" (Yalnizyan and others 1994: 36). By the mid-1970s, changes in federal tax policies that produced lower revenues led to the emergence of a federal deficit that helped to stimulate criticism of "excessive" social spending and spark support for social security measures that maintained work incentives. A number of income supplementation programs were developed provincially, and gradually many people began to be part of a cycle that saw them move from social assistance to jobs with "low pay, poor working conditions, irregular hours of work, and, therefore, high turnover" (Yalnizyan and others 1994: 39).

By the early 1980s, when a strong recession took hold in Canada, there was a notable lack of consensus about social security policy, and private-sector views were more strongly urged in the press and elsewhere. From 1982 to 1985, the Macdonald Commission, mandated by Prime Minister Trudeau, pursued various visions for a more efficient approach to social security and at one time considered a guaranteed income proposal from the Canadian Manufacturers Association that would have effectively scrapped existing social programs. The Commission's final version of a guaranteed income (Universal Income Security Program—UISP) would have collapsed most other security programs, offered a basic benefit below what a family could live on, and relied heavily on a required work provision to provide a work incentive (Kitchen 1986: 29-36). While never adopted, this right-wing version of guaranteed basic income gave the whole concept a bad name among liberals and labour groups in Canada.

National Policy Periods: The Long View

Canadian economic and social history may be examined under three "National Policy" periods. Though there are considerations that stretch the dating, these periods can be roughly dated as: 1867-1939; 1939-1974; and 1974-to date (Needham 1997).

1867-1939: The First National Policy Period

The social commitments of the First National Policy Period in Canada are those embedded in the British North America Act of 1867. The federal government was provided, under Section 91 of the Act, with the centralized control of the temporal and spatial processes of extensive growth and development. Essentially this involved getting bigger by fleshing out the country from the original British North America jurisdictions. Two pillars of the process were railway construction and immigration-encouraged population growth in the free trade area that was created. In 1879, Canadian industry became sheltered from competition by the third policy pillar, Macdonald's National Policy Tariff.

Under Section 92 of the BNA Act, the provinces and municipalities of Canada essentially undertook, in comparison to the federal responsibilities, what may be regarded as more people-based, life-cycle, or life-journey maintenance and development responsibilities, including education and hospitals. In fact Section 92 seemed to reflect the necessary practices found in more-or-less self-sufficient, unsophisticated and widely separated rural economies, in which the provision of support to those in need had to be left as the responsibility of the extended family, the church and charitable institutions, simply because they were on the spot.

Kitchen (1986) argues that the key assumption behind the Canadian approach to unemployment and poverty until 1914 was the principle of "less eligibility." The "less eligibility" principle held that if social provisioning was below what could be earned through employment there would be an incentive to work. The eligibility principle was put in place in England as a result of the work of the Poor Law Commission of 1832. It responded to the complaints of employers that the so-called Speenhamland system of poor relief met the needs of families even though no member of the family was working and to the problem of workers' increasing claims to provisioning rates that varied in proportion to family size, as a social right. It is worth emphasizing that Speenhamland was a guaranteed annual income system that worked, but foundered on its ever-increasing demands on local resources from ever-growing families. It operated from 1795 to 1834 in parts of England.

In Canada, the municipalities, some steps removed from pioneer farming communities, under Section 92 of the BNA Act had growing responsibilities for hospitals. Municipalities also provided relief as a last resort, under the condition that local residency was established, for the sick, elderly, young and for women with dependent children, but only after all family resources were exhausted.[2]

Inevitable shifts in the structure of the Canadian economy reduced the importance of once-independent agricultural communities and increased the importance of non-farm populations in growing urban areas. Employed in the production of a variety of industrial goods and services, labour force and population were increasingly made subject to the compulsions, coercions and instabilities of market-based labour relations. So the life-cycle needs of a growing industrial society created the necessity to increasingly provide more generalized social welfare.

Early in the twentieth century, social welfare policies were introduced that shifted responsibility from municipal to both provincial and federal jurisdictions. This process began in 1916, when the Province of Manitoba introduced a mothers' allowance. Rather than being unconditional, these allowances were made conditional on character references (that is, on testaments to "moral uprightness," in some sense). "Subsequently, [1920-1940] many other categories were added (veterans, unemployed, elderly, etc.) and the whole relief function has been progressively transferred to provincial and federal governments" (Armitage 1975, 1988: 271).

Overall, the period from 1867 to 1939 can be regarded as one concerned with extensive growth and development. But that period also ushered in the Great Depression that lasted the decade from 1929 through to World War II. The Depression brought an end to the expansionary forces and created debt, bankruptcy and poverty for individuals and municipalities.

1939-1974: The Second National "Progressive" Policy Period

The war brought massive intervention in market processes. The social welfare policies so greatly needed in the Depression began to be put in place during the war and the immediate postwar period to 1950. Generally, they were attempts to share more equitably and shield Canadians from the debilitating effects of the Depression, and from the social costs of market capitalism.

So, in comparison to the First National Policy Period's emphasis on extensive growth, the Second National Policy Period was concerned with intensive growth and development—how well Canadians were doing materially. To that end it also meant the design and implementation of policies that would assure greater equality of income and access to social services across the country. In terms of social welfare legislation, the Keynesian welfare state was introduced in Canada and with it the principles of equalization and universality were installed.

In tandem with social welfare reforms in Canada, the Canadian government became a signatory to the 1948 United Nations' *Universal Declaration of Human Rights* (United Nations 1948). This important document specified principles for the creation of a full democracy of human rights. In Canada, the importance of the UN UDHR is recognized in the 1997 Report of the Advisory Committee on the Changing Workplace, titled *Collective Reflection on the Changing Workplace*. Significantly, this report argues that the promotion of fairness leads to efficiency improvements.

This 1977 Report also cites Article 25 of the *Universal Declaration of Human Rights*, which says:

1. Everyone has a right to a standard of living adequate for the health and well-being of himself and of his family, including food, clothing, housing and medical care and necessary social services, and the right to security in the event of unemployment, sickness, disability, widowhood, old age or other lack of livelihood in circumstances beyond his control.

2. Motherhood and childhood are entitled to special care and assistance. All children, whether born in or out of wedlock, shall enjoy the same social protection.

As a signatory to the United Nations' *Universal Declaration of Human Rights*, Canada made a moral commitment on behalf of Canadian citizens. An unconditional BI would explicitly address that commitment.

Canada's social security advances in this period included unemployment insurance and social security. The plan to provide a social minimum was initiated in 1943 by Leonard Marsh, a Canadian public servant, and was historically linked to the plan for a postwar welfare state, advanced by Beveridge in Britain (Beveridge 1942).

The Marsh Report on Social Security (Marsh 1943, 1975) assumed a full-employment economy, and from that base the operational principles to be followed in the implementation of social security programs were to work. The principles specified by Marsh are outlined by Battle (1996: 5) and Kitchen (1986: 14):

1. social insurance programs to protect against employment earnings loss due to unemployment, illness, accident, disability, death, maternity and retirement; on scales adequate to meet the minimum needs of a single individual or a married couple;
   a) means tested social assistance for those exceptional cases not covered by social insurance.

2. national health insurance to provide all Canadians with a broad range of health services;

3. children's or family allowances to help fill the gap between wages and income needs for families with children to support; and regardless of parental income.

Interestingly, the assumption of full employment was never addressed. Government acceptance of the assumption implied that the government would countenance only frictional unemployment, that is short-term unemployment for people between jobs. Instead, the government made a weaker commitment to maintenance of a high and stable level of employment.

In the event, however, rates of unemployment in Canada have grown since the 1950s. Associated with those increases came the inevitable realization that the economic system was generating poverty. Political pressures were placed on government to implement an effective job-creation strategy. Retrospectively, it appears that so-called "natural rates of unemployment" were invented to assist attempts to remove political pressure from government. To the extent that unemployment could be seen as natural rather than systemic, the natural rate would dull awareness of poverty and suggest that poverty was natural.

But the fact of unemployment and its associated poverty could not be hidden. Support for a GAI surfaced in the 1970s. Indeed the "federal government committed itself in the early 1970's to the guaranteed income technique [but only as one of various possible schemes] as a major anti-poverty policy that would allow the greatest concentration of available resources upon those with the lowest income" (Kitchen 1986: 23-24).

In 1971 the Senate Committee on Poverty in Canada, which had been created in 1968, published its report (Canada 1971, 1976). Known as the Croll Report, it made a guaranteed income (GAI) a centrepiece proposal. The Senate Committee had been created to "investigate all aspects of poverty and recommend effective policy measures. . . . [The Report] recommended that existing programs be scrapped and replaced by a guaranteed annual income scheme.[3] As noted above, this was never implemented. In 1973, the federal government issued the *Working Paper on Social Security in Canada.* Known as the Orange Paper, it:

> was both the final flourish of the first era of social security reform in Canada, and a harbinger of the next phase. It stressed the need to meet community and individual needs through work that was socially useful, and it defined policies that could combat poverty. . . . The Orange Paper formulated a two-tiered approach to social assistance (while preserving and expanding forms of social insurance)—a guaranteed annual income scheme for those who could not work, and an income supplement for the working poor. (Yalnizyan and others 1994: 35-36)

The Second National Policy Period may be closed in 1974. In that year John Deutsch provided a proudly positive summary of what had been achieved in Canada. According to Deutsch, Canada had extended application of the equalization principle beyond the pioneering work of the early postwar period so that:

> Today there is equalization of all provincial revenues of the provinces by means of equalization payments by the federal government. An important beginning has been made on the equalization of municipal revenues as between provinces. Also there has been substantial equalization on an inter-personal basis across the country through the federal programs in health, unemployment compensation, old age assistance, welfare, etc. Recently the equalizing principle has been applied to the equalization of the price of oil across the country by means of a federal export tax. (Deutsch 1974: 9-10)

In 1974 few could see the forces that were beginning to turn back progressive social advances set in motion by the Depression and worked out during and after World War II. In fact, in 1974 Canada had already entered a Third National Policy Period that would look to undo many of the advances made in the second.

1974-to Date: The Third National "Neo-Conservative" Policy Period

This Third National Policy Period brought with it the corporatization of Canadian economic and social policy, with politicians and governments onside, and has been characterized by widespread cuts in social expenditures and increasingly constrained access for those in need of social programs. It is thought to have been ushered in, at least in part, by a crisis experienced by capitalists in their governance of labour processes. In reaction to the perceived crisis, attempts have been made by the corporate sector in all industrial nations, including Canada, to forcefully assert and reestablish their control.

The private sector placed blame for a heavy debt burden on the size of the government sector, the burden of government regulations, and the welfare state—including the principles of equality and universality. The argument ignored the fact that the welfare state and associated government expenditures and transfers to those in need had the effect of maintaining levels of income and employment at higher levels than they would otherwise have reached.

Overall the goal seems to have been the removal of state-imposed restrictions or regulations, however socially justifiable, perceived to be impeding the corporate and business sector. This focused commitment is deeply embedded in all five volumes of the report of the Macdonald Commission (*Royal Commission on the Economic Union and the*

Development Prospects for Canada—1985), which had been appointed by Prime Minister Trudeau in 1982. Chapter 19, "The Income Security System"—which outlines the Macdonald Commission's approach to a guaranteed annual income, the Universal Income Security Program (UISP)—is certainly consistent with the rhetoric of the business community of the day.[4]

The Macdonald Commission's concern with the private-sector agenda of strengthening control of labour and commodity market processes meant that its UISP proposal would only go so far as to supplement the incomes of the working poor through the tax system rather than mandate paying adequate wages. Moreover, "the Commission clearly favours de-emphasizing minimum wages as a policy device" (see note 4). In effect, the Commission was advocating a socialization of business costs by acceptance of lower wages paid to the working poor. Those low wages were to be made more livable by having society provide UISP income supplements through the tax system. But what was implicitly entailed was that, in the name of keeping business costs down, it was to be proper for business, supported by government, to shift the focus of our collective moral obligation and social responsibility to eliminate poverty among the working poor to society's shoulders.

The validity of the argument that the Commission was concerned with socializing business costs is supported first by the fact, noted by Kitchen (1986), that the Commission failed to place its UISP proposals in the context of increasing unemployment and poverty, of growing inequalities in the distribution of income, and of the breakdown in existing social programs, and second, as noted by Hum, that the Commission assumed that overall social security spending had to be held to a constant proportion of GNP. Consistently, Hum argues that:

> the Commission's case for a GAI comes not from the often stated merits for GAI, but from its fundamental presupposition that restraint must last for a long, long time, . . . its eyes seem never to shift from the deficit numbers. . . . For the Commission, it is support of market principles that will lead to economic growth. We are now in a position to see the Commission's twofold position: hold the line, and beneath this, a disguised trickle down theory. (see note 4)

The principle of universality came under attack in so far as the UISP proposal would have eliminated the universal family allowance system. Unemployment insurance was also to be eliminated. Kitchen (1986: 34) suggests that UISP would have contributed to the institutionalization of poverty, in some cases at lower support levels than available in existing programs. All in all, the Macdonald Commission's call for a so-called guaranteed income, titled *Universal Income Security Program* or UISP, was a political non-starter, a proposal going nowhere.[5] A great many Canadians were left with negative feelings toward the idea of a basic income.

And So . . .

Over the historical sweep of the three National Policy periods, Canadian governments have had a checkered and often reluctant history in terms of commitments to progressive reform of the economic system. Some battles seemed to have been won, for a variety of progressive policy programs were put in place, particularly in the period 1940-1974. In the last twenty years or so, however, welfare and other social agencies have been fighting to hold onto what they had gained and have been unable to effectively look for improvements. With social programs cut back and made more restrictive in their application, it seems the once-won battles have to be fought again.

Now, however, with growing recognition and admission of Canadian social problems such as homelessness and child poverty, progressive reform that would pick up where the Second National Policy Period was abruptly truncated can perhaps resume. On one side, technical efficiency is an obvious goal of each business enterprise as it searches for institutional income security through the maintenance and growth of its profit-earning capacities. On the other side, the technical efficiency processes and contingent-workforce strategies employed by businesses can result in growing social inefficiencies or social costs. These social costs are of a wide variety, from unemployment, to poverty, ill-health and, generally, unfulfilled human potential.

Clearly the search for greater stability and income security for business has created instability in income security for many individuals. Income security for individuals, such as that provided by an adequate BI, is itself a stabilizing device for society that will also increase income security for businesses as they strive to make the flexible workforce the employment norm. It will be interesting to see how long it takes the private sector to realize this.

4

A Canadian Basic Income: Needed, Justified and Beneficial

> "Putting the work ethic at the centre of the welfare state" has been demonstrated to be an inappropriate slogan. The work ethic—in the sense of the motivation to work long hours in physically or mentally demanding toil, as an investment for future wealth—is certainly still relevant for the expansion of the world economy and the improvement of the welfare of the great majority of its inhabitants. But in those post-industrial economies that rely primarily on capital- and information-intensive production and on the financial sector for their share of global markets, the puritan ethic of hard work can be counterproductive, if it leads to a blaming attitude toward those for whom there are no longer roles in traditional industries, or to costly social divisions, punitive policies and a breakdown of trust and cooperation that are necessary conditions for prosperity and good democratic governance.
>
> — Bill Jordan, *The New Politics of Welfare*

CANADA'S SOCIAL-SECURITY POLICY PATH can be characterized as increasingly conflicted, moving from European-style social democratic attitudes that supported investment in community well-being and the universality that made this politically accceptable (late 1930s to early 1970s) toward increasing infatuation with the so-called tougher U.S. stance of the past two decades. The U.S. model favoured targeted social spending, yet widened the gap between rich and poor while holding down official unemployment figures by proliferating low-wage (below the poverty line) McJobs. In Canada also, the gap between rich and poor has widened, the middle class is losing ground, more jobs are low-paid and precarious, and unemployment, hovering currently at around 7-8 percent, remains a persistent problem (Yalnizyan 1998). Since Statistics Canada does not routinely count people who have given up looking for work, it is likely that Canada's real rate of unemployment is close to double the official figure.

Without again detailing the gradual erosion of Canada's commitment to a comprehensive social security system between the mid-1980s and the end of the 1990s, it can be said that the federal governments of the period increased the wealth of the rich at the expense of the poor, withdrew support from the national unemployment insurance system and generally created an atmosphere of insecurity and anxiety about the unemployment safety net. At the same time, both the public and private sectors were busily reengineering, downsizing, rightsizing—creating increasing numbers of unemployed, underemployed and insecurely employed (Stewart 1998; McQuaig 1998, 1995, 1993). As well, during the mid- to late 1990s, the deficit was presented as Problem Number One for Canada, overshadowing every other concern except "global competitiveness" and requiring yet further constraint in social spending. Only in 1998 was this message changed slightly to reflect federal and provincial governments' desire to garner recognition for "taming the deficit."

It is against this backdrop of individual anxiety about downward mobility, incessant media promotion of the urgent need for fiscal restraint and the evils of "welfare cheats," and an increasing polarization between haves and have-nots that we must view the challenge of gaining Canadian acceptance of the concept of a BI. While the pendulum appears to be swinging slightly back toward an understanding that social cohesion depends on social investment, it will require a suspension of deeply held beliefs for many Canadians to think calmly about a BI as a response to the fundamental changes we are experiencing.

How might Canadians be encouraged to discuss BI as a practical approach to dealing with the new realities we face? Perhaps the best way is to summarize the arguments in favour of a BI. With these up on the wall in plain view, discussion can begin! This chapter details those arguments: why Canada needs a BI, why a BI is fair and justifiable and what positive benefits a BI promises, even beyond preventing human suffering and social unrest.

Why Canada Needs a BI

- *Canada needs a BI because no societal responses currently under serious discussion in Canada are fully adequate to deal with long-term structural unemployment, underemployment and the private sector's insistent demand for a flexible workforce.*

While there is still strong public resistance in Canada to abandoning the vulnerable and less able in society, there has been an unrelenting effort to "manufacture consent" for substantial reductions in social security expenditures and a much-heralded switch "from passive to active" social support, that is, from welfare for the long-term unemployed to skills training for this group and income supplements for those who do secure employment. There is nothing intrinsically wrong with this tack. But to continue to blame those made redundant by smart machines and global employment restructuring is not acceptable.

Politicians praise training together with some type of on-the-job experience as the ultimate cure for unemployment and poverty. Bureaucratic insiders laughingly call this the "field of dreams" solution—train the people and the jobs will come! Training may be key in the short term for matching suitable people and some types of jobs, such as those that involve the latest high-tech skills or hands-on personal service. But there is some suspicion, even among those responsible for designing and implementing each new round of skills training, that over the longer term the hottest job market to emerge may be for trainers.

Upgrading basic literacy, numeracy and computer skills can be viewed with more favour than specific training for jobs that may never materialize or may disappear from Canada, since such upgrading can be put to good use in living and lifelong learning. But there are concerns about raising the hopes for immediate employment of those in any training program without some certainty of their subsequently finding secure, adequately waged jobs.

Recently, the pressure to admit more well-educated immigrants to Canada—supposedly to fill jobs that go begging because of a skills gap in Canada between training and skills needed by employers—has raised questions about whether this gap is real or whether immigrants will simply work for less than Canadians with comparable education. If there is a skills-jobs match problem, addressing it should be a straightforward government and private-sector priority. But rapid technological change coupled with continuing demands for a flexible work force mean that governments are always playing catch-up, employers do turn to skilled immigrants, and many Canadians doubt whether they will ever have a secure livelihood under the new rules.

A BI would help to spread around any jobs that materialize and would assure everyone a decent living. *Canada needs a BI primarily because we need alternative approaches to distributing paid employment, goods and services.* It is imperative now for decision makers to consult with the public about BI as a fair, cost-effective way to do this in light of our goals for the future of Canadian society.

* *Canada needs a BI because, while the welfare state was a notable post-World War II accomplishment, no less for Canada and the U.S. than for the Europeans, it was created to provide a safety net for postwar industrial workers with certain stable employment patterns. And times have changed.*

The creators of a BI scenario for Ireland put it this way:

> The relevance of the Keynes-Beveridge model of the modern welfare state, where one wage earner per family was enough to support a decent standard of living, where workers stayed with one company most of their working lives and where the state provided short-term assistance for those who needed immediate help, has almost disappeared. . . . [In the global economy of the 1990s] labour flexibility has replaced job security, lifelong learning has replaced lifelong employment, and unskilled workers are competing with lower wage workers in Eastern Europe and the Third World. (Clark and Healy 1997: 1-2)

A December 1993 report for the Canadian Government and Competitiveness Project suggested that the major problems with the income security system in Canada at that time were

> the existence of a "welfare trap" that discourages self-sufficiency and contributes to the perpetuation of poverty; the seemingly uncontrollable growth of welfare costs and the increased strain on debt-burdened federal and provincial governments; and, the presence of an unnecessarily complex system that is costly to administer, often poorly targeted to the needy, and inequitable to such groups as the working poor. (Grady and others 1995: 62-63)

Welfare costs have been slashed, primarily because eligibility requirements have been tightened, but the system is still costly, complex and essentially a poverty trap. It too often leaves "beneficiaries" with no recourse but the food bank, no place to hide from the humiliation of the system's probing.

BI allows society to deal with the growing infeasibility of a generous welfare state for which the conditions can no longer be guaranteed— stable, adequately waged employment for almost all males. BI spreads the work, allowing engagement and participation in society for all, even without the kind of post-World War II full employment that made the one-earner middle-class household a norm for three decades. *We need a BI to move today's Canadian governments beyond fighting yesterday's welfare battles.*

- *Canada needs a BI to maintain social cohesion during the transition to a fundamentally changed world of work. A society that excludes many of its members from full citizenship puts itself at risk.*

The extent to which many existing kinds of waged work must be, should be and will be phased out is still extremely controversial. It is very difficult for most people to envision a society where relatively fewer workers are needed to mine natural resources (but can fewer men down the shafts be a bad thing?), manufacture goods (will assembly lines be missed?) and provide routine services (how stimulating was life in the typing pool?). Yet there are increasingly clear signs that such a world is taking shape, and slowly we are beginning to understand its pitfalls and possibilities.

New kinds of jobs will materialize—it's already happening as twenty-somethings start their own multimedia production companies and home-delivered gourmet meals fly out of new catering establishments. But we don't know how soon, how much or what kind of work this will be—though it will almost certainly, at least in the fifty-year near term, be less secure and more contingent for a majority of Canadians than were the good jobs of the 1950s, 1960s and 1970s. For people with no postsecondary education or training, the prospects for earning an adequate living are especially bleak.

Wise people make plans for the contingencies of uncertain times. We must prod our governments to take action and then work with them to design new approaches, such as the BI, to address the challenge of maintaining social cohesion as we adapt to new patterns of employment and to the steady-state constraints of environmental sustainability. Since we cannot continue growth that degrades the environment, employment should no longer be tied mainly to production for the market. *A BI is needed to prevent a win-lose polarization of society and avoid creating a permanent underclass during this fundamental societal transition.*

Why a Canadian BI Is Justified

- *It is immoral to stigmatize and penalize people who cannot find enough paid work to support themselves and their families, and to participate fully in community life.* There is no real moral or socially viable alternative to some form of BI if society cannot ensure secure, adequately waged jobs for all who want them. Adequate income, together with social provision of the necessary means for well-being, is a human right recognized by Canada when it signed the *Universal Declaration of Human Rights* in 1948. This assumes the right to a sufficient minimum income either through guaranteed employment, guaranteed income or a combination of these. Without a minimum guaranteed resource base, many people will remain highly vulnerable and dependent on the charity and goodwill of others.

- *An ethical argument for an unconditional BI can be based on the central assumption that having a job has positive utility for the job holder.* And if a few people withdraw from competition for jobs, this will benefit rather than damage society, since there are not enough jobs to go around anyway (Daly and Cobb 1989).

- *"Economic democracy" requires that all citizens have sufficient resources to make uncoerced economic decisions.* This requires a BI so people can turn down undesired jobs. A BI offers more choice under capitalism: you can live at the minimum, go after more money, take a job you like part time or at low pay; dirty, dangerous, dumb jobs would need to pay more.

- *BI is a rightful dividend for taxpayers' social investment in health, law and order, education, research and development, and infrastructure over many decades.* It is this social investment that has made possible the current technology-based prosperity enjoyed by the private sector (Alperovitz 1994). In fact, it is this social investment together with enormous outlays of unpaid labour that underpins the prosperity of the formal economic market structure. The fact that this prosperity will depend less and less on the paid labour of taxpayers requires redress. BI is that redress, and would constitute recognition of the extent to which the success of a society depends centrally on the contributions and well-being of all its citizens.

- *Because the earth is the heritage of all, it is right that all should benefit from use of it. BI constitutes land rents to the landless and user fees for private-sector use of natural resources.* This is considered a wildly radical justification of BI by everyone who has been socialized to accept the current socio-economic arrangements regarding ownership and rights to use of natural resources, including air and water as pollution sinks. But it is considered a valid argument by some (Van Parijs 1992) and does have a certain compelling quality of fairness.

The Positive Benefits a BI Offers Canadians

- *A BI can serve as the keystone of a new set of social arrangements to ensure each individual's economic security, opportunities for meaningful work and engagement in family and community life.* With BI as a foundation, new ways of living and working can be considered: shorter work weeks/years, sabbatical leaves, lifelong learning, community service, even more time for the kids.
- *A well-designed BI promotes widespread employment and fights poverty traps—that is, improves the work incentive structure at the lower end of the income distribution—since BI is not taxed nor is it withdrawn when additional money is earned.* A BI would also make it much easier to employ people—allow them to participate in society—in environmentally benign ways. A BI would be an incentive for paid and unpaid work to be shared more fairly and could, coupled as it should be with a minimum wage, open up employment for the low-skilled while giving them sufficient income to participate in society. A BI also encourages enterprise and self-employment, the entrepreneurial risk-taking that our society values so highly.
- *A BI facilitates the growth of different kinds of useful non-market work and of productive time for personal development; both activities complement paid work in the era of the flexible workforce.* The fact that more people will choose to study or pursue idealistic or artistic endeavours will benefit society in the long run; if some withdraw from paid work, there will be more for those who want it.
- *A BI maintains consumer demand in the face of unemployment, contingent employment and inadequate wages.*
- *A BI substantially reduces transaction costs and increases transparency by allowing most of the complex and costly welfare bureaucracy to be dismantled.*

But can we afford a BI for Canadians? One model of how we could is offered in the next chapter.

A Canadian Basic Income Model

World's Richest 6M Get Richer (May 17, 1999)

The world's estimated 6 million millionaires have shrugged off the effects of last year's financial turmoil and are getting richer by the day.

New research by Merrill Lynch, the investment bank, with Gemini Consulting, a management consultancy, found the wealth held by high net worth individuals with more than $1m of financial assets grew last year by 12 per cent to $21,600bn.

The *World Wealth Report* produced by the two firms projects a steady rise to $32,700bn by the end of 2003—a growth rate which is expected to attract more firms into the lucrative market for private banking and wealth management services.

This year's estimates suggest the rich are, in fact, richer than had been thought. Estimates have been revised upwards by around $2,000bn, in the light of new data from the US and Germany showing wealth is concentrated in fewer hands than was supposed.

— George Graham, *Financial Times*

WE HAVE SEEN THAT A BI can serve as the foundation upon which to build a richer, more human way of life. Entrepreneurial activity will be encouraged and everyone can share what waged work there is, with their basic needs secured. People will be free to devote more energy to family concerns, community service, learning and self-development. In time, as people begin to lead more balanced lives, societal perceptions will adjust to recognize the value of these varied activities and accord recognition appropriately for the many kinds of good work that income security permits.

Deciding how to finance a BI will be a central component of public debate about the concept. The question has been considered in a number of countries as well as here, and current ideas focus on a range of possibilities: savings from collapsing most of the social service bureaucracy, a Tobin tax on currency speculation (ul Haq and others 1996), a very small "bit tax" on all electronic transactions (Cordell and Ide 1997), a variety of changes to income and corporate taxes and user-pay charges on use of non-renewable resources. It is hard to imagine that the ingenious armies of economists and accountants will fail to come up with a feasible means, once the desired end result is specified. The Irish are showing the way with a recently completed set of financing plans for a national basic income (Clark and Healy 1997). It's time for policymakers across the globe to consider BI and to evaluate national models.

What a Basic Income in Canada Might Look Like

A BI society, with its universality and security, provides both an effective social safety net and labour market flexibility. The other options being considered by governments (traditional strong welfare state or workfare-type reforms) in the advanced capitalist countries offer one or the other, income security or labour-market flexibility, usually trading off a bit of one for a little more of the other. These options do not offer attractive alternatives, for they frequently, in essence, pit the social classes against each other, with income security benefiting those at the lower end of the economic ladder, while a reduced welfare state based on a minimal workfare program benefits through reduced tax rates those who are already well off. With its ability to offer both income security and labour-market flexibility, BI gets beyond this trade-off, providing a means by which all Canadians will be able to benefit from the wealth being created by the new economy.

Yet one cannot examine the issues around a BI too closely without looking at an actual BI proposal.[1] BI is a generic term that fits many different types of proposals (or at least is applied to many proposals). The main differences are twofold: (1) different levels of benefits—from a full BI, with benefit levels set at the official poverty level, to a partial BI set at a lower level; and (2) how the BI will be funded. Most BI proposals include a flat income tax as their sole or primary source of funding. (Such a funding mechanism is not an essential aspect of BI; other sources of revenue, noted above, can be considered.)

Yet a flat income tax is used because it is the easiest source of tax revenues for the person developing a BI proposal to estimate and model. As these proposals have been, for the most part, developed by individuals and groups with very limited resources, this is their only option. Were a system to be developed by either a government agency or a well-endowed research institute, alternative modes of taxation could easily be developed, and the tax on income could be dramatically reduced.

For the purpose of furthering the discussion on BI in Canada we have developed a rudimentary BI system for Canada. The system is designed to replace the majority of Canada's social welfare and income assistance programs. In this chapter we present this proposal, along with some analysis of its effects on income distribution. We have developed this BI scenario for Canada not as an actual proposal, but as a hypothetical proposal that allows the issues raised by a BI proposal to be discussed. Much further work, requiring resources beyond those at our disposable, would be required to develop a complete Canadian BI proposal. The purpose of this book is to help generate this discussion, with the hope that it will eventually lead to dedication of the necessary resources to construct such a proposal.[2]

Hypothetical Canadian BI system

Our hypothetical BI system would replace the existing programs of social welfare and income assistance. It is funded and paid out at the federal level, thus relieving the provinces and territories of this obligation. As it does not account for those currently receiving disability benefits, this would remain an obligation for the provinces and territories. As this obligation is a small fraction of the current obligations for social welfare and assistance, the provinces and territories would be able to fund disability payments at their existing levels. The federal government would continue to provide Canada Health and Social Transfer (CHST) funding at the 1999/2000 levels. This level of funding is currently earmarked for both health expenditures and public assistance. As the level will remain the same, the provinces and territories will have additional funds (money earmarked for social welfare, which is now replaced with the BI) that could be used for improving the health care and education systems, or for reducing tax rates.

Payment Levels

Our hypothetical BI system would include the following annual payments. These payments are universal, based on citizenship or permanent residency (Canadian resident for more than five years), and are not means tested (see table 5.1). This means that every Canadian sixty-five and over would receive annually a payment of $7,000, regardless of their income, with adults receiving $5,000 and children receiving $3,000 (paid to their primary caregiver, in most cases their mother). The household payment of $5,000 is to be divided equally among all those twenty-one and older living in the household.

Table 5.1
Basic Income payment levels

Age	Payment
Elderly (65+)	$7,000
Adult (21-64)	5,000
Child	3,000
Household	5,000

Cost of the Basic Income Proposal

The costs of our hypothetical BI system—$198.6 billion—are calculated by multiplying the BI payment by the number of individuals in each age category. These costs are provided in table 5.2 below. Population projections for 1999 are derived from Statistics Canada's projections for 2001.

Table 5.2
Costs of Basic Income payments

Age	Population (thousands)	BI payment (dollars)	Total costs (thousands)
Elderly (65+)	3,794.4	$7,000	$26,560,800
Adults (21-64)	18,758.0	5,000	93,790,000
Children	8,047.9	3,000	24,143,700
Sub-total	30,600.3		
Households*	10,820.1	5,000	54,100,500
Total			$198,595,000

* Number of households
Source: Budget 1999, Dept. of Finance, Canada. C. Clark population estimates.

Total Costs of Federal Government

Our BI system is funded and paid out at the level of the federal government. Under this BI system, most of what the federal government does would remain the same, except that the transfers to persons would be replaced by the BI system. In table 5.3 we have the federal budget, as contained in their 1999/2000 budget proposal.

Table 5.3
Existing federal spending, 1999/2000
(billions)

Transfers to persons	$36.9
Transfers to other gov't.	20.4
Direct program spending	18.6
Crown corporations	3.9
Defence	8.7
Other	22.7
Debt servicing	42.5
Total	$153.7

Source: Budget 1999, Dept. of Finance,
        Canada

Savings Resulting from a BI System

Because a BI system would relieve the provinces and territories of one of their major obligations, as well as provide relief to the federal government, there will be some savings under a BI system. In table 5.4 we give only the most obvious savings. A more detailed examination of the government budgets will, most likely, reveal other government expenditures on income support or income assistance programs that are buried in other government budget lines. Furthermore, the system of equalization payments could possibly be reexamined in light of the income distribution effects of a BI system. This leaves other federal government expenditures of $116.8 billion. Add this to the above calculated cost of the BI system of $198.6 billion and the federal government expenditures for 1999/2000 total $315.4 billion.

Table 5.4
Savings generated by a Basic Income system
(billions)

Savings	1999/2000
Transfers to persons	$36.9
Total	$36.9

Source: Budget 1999, Dept. of Finance, Canada

Revenue

The BI system being examined here replaces the existing federal income tax system with a flat tax on all incomes except corporate profits, which are taxed at the current rate. This is only one type of taxation system that a BI system could use, and as mentioned above, is used more for the sake of simplicity than for any other reason. The employment insurance premium is also eliminated. Other existing taxes are kept in place. The existing federal tax system for 1999/2000 is given below in table 5.5.

Table 5.5
Existing federal government revenue system
(billions)

Personal income tax	$75.0
Corporate income tax	20.9
Other	2.9
Employment Insurance premiums	18.3
Consumption taxes	32.3
Non-tax revenue	7.5
Total	$157.0
Taxes eliminated under BI	
Personal income tax	($75.0)
Employment Insurance premiums	(18.3)
Remaining tax revenue	$63.6

Source: Budget 1999, Dept. of Finance, Canada, and
C. Clark's calculations

With tax revenue of $63.6 billion, the new BI system must raise $251.8 billion in tax revenue to produce a balanced budget. This will be raised with a flat tax on all incomes (except corporate profits, which are taxed at current rates).

Given a level taxable income of $608.1 billion and total federal government spending (minus existing tax revenue of $63.6 billion) of $251.8 billion, the necessary flat tax for this BI system is: 251.8/608.1 = 41.41 percent. This is a conservative estimate. National income estimates frequently miss income that would be taxable under a BI system (such as capital gains), thus the actual tax rate would most likely be significantly lower.

Effects on Provinces' and Territories' Spending and Revenue

The hypothetical BI system developed here would replace all social welfare and assistance spending with the exception of disability payments, for which the current system is retained. Further work is necessary to fully integrate the national BI system with the provinces' and territories' taxing and spending systems. Clearly the levels of spending and taxation of the provinces and territories will need to be adjusted to take into account these changes. Since a BI system greatly reduces the need for many provincial and territorial programs, there will

Table 5.6
Projected taxable income, 1999/2000[a]
(billions)

Wages, salaries	$490.1
Corporate profits	83.3
Government businesses	8.3
Interest misc.	47.7
Farm	2.6
Non-farm	59.4
Total	$691.4
Minus	
Corporate profits	-83.3
Taxable total	$608.1

Source: C. Clark's calculations
a Income levels for 1999/2000 are projected at
a rate of 4% above 1998/1999 levels.

be scope for increases in health expenditures and tax cuts, as well as other spending changes based on the needs of each province or territory.

Distribution Effects

With any BI system, as with any change in tax and benefits, there are necessarily winners and losers. We show the winners and losers in tables 5.7a-f below, using the hypothetical household method used by the federal government in their most recent (1999/2000) budget. It should be remembered that the BI flat tax is on earned income only. The BI payment is always tax free. The after-tax income 1999/2000 is the projection of the impact of the current federal income tax system, as given in the 1999/2000 federal budget. From these tables we can see that there are clear benefits to those with low incomes, as well as for the elderly and for families. It should be noted that the accuracy of these comparisons is dependent on the accuracy of the federal budget 1999/2000 projections. A BI system as given here includes a flat tax, which means the elimination of all current deductions and tax credits. Because such deductions and tax credits are often not included in hypothetical household projections, these tend to underestimate incomes of the upper-income households. Thus it is possible that the losses at the top-income categories would be higher. The effective tax rate for each hypothetical household indicates that the BI system presented here is progressive, in that the rate of taxes out of total income goes up as income goes up. Thus, although the BI system presented here relies on a flat tax, it is progressive in its total impact on the household.

Table 5.7a
Typical single individual

Income	After-tax income 1999/2000	BI income	Flat tax under BI system	Total income under BI	Gain or (loss)
7,500	7,717	10,000	3,106	14,394	6,677
10,000	9,869	10,000	4,141	15,859	5,990
15,000	14,108	10,000	6,212	18,789	4,681
20,000	18,312	10,000	8,282	21,718	3,406
25,000	22,517	10,000	10,353	24,648	2,131
30,000	26,481	10,000	12,423	27,577	1,096
35,000	30,136	10,000	14,494	30,507	371
40,000	33,873	10,000	16,564	33,436	-437
45,000	37,573	10,000	18,635	36,366	-1,208
50,000	41,272	10,000	20,705	39,295	-1,977
55,000	44,972	10,000	22,776	42,225	-2,748
60,000	48,649	10,000	24,846	45,154	-3,495
65,000	52,184	10,000	26,917	48,084	-4,101
75,000	59,139	10,000	31,058	53,943	-5,197
100,000	76,527	10,000	41,410	68,590	-7,937

col. 4 = col. 1 x 41.41%; col. 5 = cols. 3 - 4 + 1; col. 6 = cols. 5 - 2

Table 5.7b
Typical one-earner family of four

Income	After-tax income 1999/2000	BI income	Flat tax under BI system	Total income under BI	Gain or (loss)
13,500	18,071	21,000	5,590	28,910	10,839
15,000	19,403	21,000	6,212	29,789	10,386
20,000	23,608	21,000	8,282	32,718	9,110
25,000	27,008	21,000	10,353	35,648	8,640
30,000	30,047	21,000	12,423	38,577	8,530
35,000	33,303	21,000	14,494	41,507	8,204
40,000	36,636	21,000	16,564	44,436	7,800
45,000	40,086	21,000	18,635	47,366	7,280
50,000	43,536	21,000	20,705	50,295	6,759
55,000	46,986	21,000	22,776	53,225	6,239
60,000	50,411	21,000	24,846	56,154	5,743
65,000	53,711	21,000	26,917	59,084	5,373
75,000	60,219	21,000	31,058	64,943	4,724
100,000	77,607	21,000	41,410	79,590	1,983

col. 4 = col. 1 x 41.41%; col. 5 = cols. 3 - 4 + 1; col. 6 = cols. 5 - 2

Table 5.7c
Typical two-earner family of four

Income	After-tax income 1999/2000	BI income	Flat tax under BI system	Total income under BI	Gain or (loss)
20,000	24,296	21,000	8,282	32,718	8,422
25,000	28,657	21,000	10,353	35,648	6,991
30,000	32,373	21,000	12,423	38,577	6,204
35,000	35,584	21,000	14,494	41,507	5,923
40,000	39,196	21,000	16,564	44,436	5,240
45,000	42,922	21,000	18,635	47,366	4,444
50,000	46,840	21,000	20,705	50,295	3,455
55,000	50,525	21,000	22,776	53,225	2,700
60,000	54,210	21,000	24,846	56,154	1,944
65,000	57,888	21,000	26,917	59,084	1,196
75,000	65,192	21,000	31,058	64,943	-250
100,000	84,213	21,000	41,410	79,590	-4,623

col. 4 = col. 1 x 41.41%; col. 5 = cols. 3 - 4 + 1; col. 6 = cols. 5 - 2

Table 5.7d
Typical single parent with one child

Income	After-tax income 1999/2000	BI income	Flat tax under BI system	Total income under BI	Gain or (loss)
10,000	12,623	13,000	4,141	18,859	6,236
15,000	17,478	13,000	6,212	21,789	4,311
20,000	22,095	13,000	8,282	24,718	2,623
25,000	26,392	13,000	10,353	27,648	1,256
30,000	30,042	13,000	12,423	30,577	535
35,000	33,439	13,000	14,494	33,507	68
40,000	36,803	13,000	16,564	36,436	-367
45,000	40,378	13,000	18,635	39,366	-1,013
50,000	43,950	13,000	20,705	42,295	-1,655
55,000	47,528	13,000	22,776	45,225	-2,304
60,000	51,102	13,000	24,846	48,154	-2,948
65,000	54,622	13,000	26,917	51,084	-3,539
75,000	61,437	13,000	31,058	56,943	-4,495
100,000	78,825	13,000	41,410	71,590	-7,235

col. 4 = col. 1 x 41.41%; col. 5 = cols. 3 - 4 + 1; col. 6 = cols. 5 - 2

Table 5.7e
Typical elderly single

Income	After-tax income 1999/2000	BI income	Flat tax under BI system	Total income under BI	Gain or (loss)
12,500	12,653	12,000	5,176	19,324	6,671
15,000	14,729	12,000	6,212	20,789	6,060
20,000	18,878	12,000	8,282	23,718	4,840
25,000	23,029	12,000	10,353	26,648	3,619
30,000	26,833	12,000	12,423	29,577	2,744
35,000	30,306	12,000	14,494	32,507	2,201
40,000	33,878	12,000	16,564	35,436	1,558
45,000	37,451	12,000	18,635	38,366	915
50,000	41,046	12,000	20,705	41,295	249
55,000	44,547	12,000	22,776	44,225	-323
60,000	47,692	12,000	24,846	47,154	-538
65,000	50,714	12,000	26,917	50,084	-631
75,000	56,626	12,000	31,058	55,943	-684
100,000	72,768	12,000	41,410	70,590	-2,178

col. 4 = col. 1 x 41.41%; col. 5 = cols. 3 - 4 + 1; col. 6 = cols. 5 - 2

Table 5.7f
Typical elderly couple

Income	After-tax income 1999/2000	BI income	Flat tax under BI system	Total income under BI	Gain or (loss)
20,000	20,398	19,000	8,282	30,718	10,320
25,000	24,813	19,000	10,353	33,648	8,835
30,000	28,793	19,000	12,423	36,577	7,784
35,000	32,615	19,000	14,494	39,507	6,892
40,000	36,188	19,000	16,564	42,436	6,248
45,000	39,760	19,000	18,635	45,366	5,606
50,000	43,333	19,000	20,705	48,295	4,962
55,000	46,925	19,000	22,776	51,225	4,300
60,000	50,435	19,000	24,846	54,154	3,719
65,000	53,580	19,000	26,917	57,084	3,504
75,000	59,602	19,000	31,058	62,943	3,341
100,000	75,216	19,000	41,410	77,590	2,374

col. 4 = col. 1 x 41.41%; col. 5 = cols. 3 - 4 + 1; col. 6 = cols. 5 - 2

Let's Play a New Mind Game . . . How to Create a Future that Works for Canada

*I*N THIS BOOK, we have tried to make clear why Canada *needs* a Basic Income program, why a Canadian BI is *justified* and what *positive benefits* a BI will have for Canada. So . . . if we, and perhaps you, think that Canada should take the lead in making BI the foundation of an economic strategy to address our contemporary great transformation and provide a better quality of life, what can we do to make it happen?

- We can become better informed about our governments' sources of income and spending patterns. There are alternatives, as shown by the *Alternative Federal Budget Papers 1998* (Canadian Centre for Policy Alternatives and Choices 1998). The detailed BI models prepared for Ireland (Clark and Healy 1997) and the example of a Canadian BI in chapter 5 of this book suggest how budget alternatives might accommodate a BI.

- We can challenge the idea that BI is some kind of far-fetched utopian dream by talking with our friends and co-workers, people in our faith groups and clubs. The discussion guide at the end of this book is meant to help get conversations up and running. We can also create dialogue by writing letters to newspapers and short articles for their Op-Ed pages.

If a flexible workforce is what the world now wants—and 45 percent of employed Canadians are currently in non-standard jobs—we can discuss BI as the key to *positive flexibility*. A well-designed BI would mean more real choice of jobs, and higher pay for the most unpleasant jobs in society. There would be useful work for all and recognition of the value of the many kinds of work that keep society healthy. Poverty traps would disappear, civil unrest be prevented and consumer spending maintained among the people most likely to contribute to strong local economies.

- We can give serious thought to how best to prepare the soil to grow support for a BI. What is the needed societal mix of reassurance and challenge? Certainly a societal commitment—at all levels of government—to provide people with secure access to affordable housing, and adequate food, health care, education and recreation is key to people welcoming a BI approach to meeting their basic needs.

Equally important, people will need a vision of the options for a fuller, more varied life that BI can open up to them—more time for parenting, community service, self-development through music and art, environmental projects, assisting teachers, the possibilities are nearly infinite—as well as the opportunity to participate in decisions about what investments in community life and well-being should be made in a BI society.

Before people can accept the realities of what the flexible workforce entails—and BI as a positive way of dealing with them—they need reassurance that they, and others, would still be able to stay connected, engaged, rewarded and able to find meaning and self-esteem in a life that might not revolve around a 9-to-5 paid job. And they need to understand that BI in no way rules out full-time, adequately waged employment, but rather softens the loss of its availability to all.

- We need to ensure a bountiful harvest of benefits from a Canadian BI by publicly demanding that our elected officials—too many currently in denial—address the challenge of the changing nature of work. As their constituents, we must hold them accountable for fulfilling the long-term societal commitments in which a BI program must be embedded if it is to promote positive changes in the lives of people and their communities. Access to health care, food, housing, education and child care must be seen as fundamental rights that, together with BI, enable people to construct meaningful lives, and livelihoods, in the fast-changing world.

- To ensure a positive BI harvest, we need to initiate education for community engagement and self-development. Beginning in early childhood, this would emphasize doing and being through useful work as well as the arts, music and other forms of expression. We need to influence and shape our educational systems to foster questioning, exploration, problem solving, individual initiative, community service and cooperative projects.

- As BI advocates, we need to encourage visions of a way of life that offers more security and leisure than the current anxious and time-starved routine in which many people find themselves. With more varied daily life possible because of the BI, adults of all ages will gradually make engagement in useful and stimulating activities a family way of life. It is not too utopian to imagine that gardening, environmental protection, community clean-ups, service to seniors and myriad more active rather than passive activities will largely replace TV and video games as sources of enjoyment. As well, people less exhausted by the rat race will have less need to "veg out."

Those who choose to live simply with less income in a BI society will find many models. The phenomenal success of the book *Your Money or Your Life* (Dominguez and Robin, 1992) and other guides to voluntary simplicity suggest that a substantial minority of people in affluent societies are ready for this change. Such current rediscoveries as co-housing, LETS-type barter operations, bicycling, community gardens, local computer access and recycling building materials and clothes all testify to the possibility of creating better living through less materialism and more sharing.

Key to this change has been the idea of sustainable communities, which has travelled and found advocates. With it has come the vision of more self-reliance—for people and their communities: more homegrown food and locally produced products, more self-maintained health through prevention, more sports and entertainment involving local people rather than packaged for them, more community cooperation to put community capital to work to realize community goals.

• These are some of the things that Canadians can do to bring BI to public attention, help move it onto the political agenda, and ensure that the required social commitment exists to prevent BI from seeming to be, or becoming, just "a cheque in the mail." These are some of the ways that we can work to assure the equitability and economic security that we believe are everyone's rights in our affluent society.

BASIC INCOME: A DISCUSSION GUIDE

This brief guide offers suggestions for encouraging discussion of the desirability and feasibility of a Basic Income (BI) for Canada.

THE TYPE OF BASIC INCOME under consideration here is the one currently most discussed in Europe, Britain, New Zealand and elsewhere. It would be *universal, unconditional* and *adequate to live decently,* provided there are societal commitments to affordable housing, and quality child care, education and health care. A higher amount would be provided for people with disabilities and the elderly, who would have difficulty augmenting their incomes through paid employment. Expect that some people will want to talk about variations on this generic BI model.

• Why do some people believe that a Canadian BI is needed at this particular time?

Considering this question might involve thinking about some of the following questions:

- What is the current outlook for adequately waged, secure employment over the next several decades and beyond?
- Why are employers calling for a flexible workforce and what do they mean by this?
- What is it like to be an employee in the flexible workforce?

That is, what do some people like about temporary, contract and part-time work? What is the downside of this flexible workforce for other people?

- What might be some positive opportunities for people in the flexible workforce if they had basic economic security?

One of the main reasons for the fall in full-time and increase in part-time employment is the amount of work now being contracted out by companies. This increase in flexibility of the workforce is being seen

54

primarily as negative by social commentators, but could be positive if a few guarantees were in place. Flexibility of hiring can give people the option to take what work they want and give them more control over their working time. However, under the present system, contract workers do not have the same rights as other full-time employees. The rights of contract workers will have to be secured, along with benefits of a decent level to reflect the greater vulnerability to periods of insufficient work. A basic income would provide that security. (Merry 1997:73)

• *Do people see any problems with a universal BI?*

Fears about wasting money by providing a BI to the well-off will need discussion in the context of the costs and benefits of targetting BI. People may want to talk about the pros and cons of BI going to each individual rather than to each family, and about details of a BI for children and youth.

• *What concerns do people have about an unconditional BI?*

Concerns about BI promoting idleness, the inequity of people free riding and just plain political unacceptability will need discussion. Many people who might otherwise be BI advocates are genuinely concerned that if no one were forced to work for a living, many would do nothing, losing structure and meaning in their lives.

It will be important to talk about how different ways of educating children and youth enable people to discover the satisfaction of developing their unique talents and of taking part in community and other service work as a matter of course.

People may want to discuss the extent to which it is true that almost everyone potentially has something positive to offer the community, and how best to tap into this potential.

• *What are some of the arguments against the idea of a BI for Canada?*

Besides worries about universality and unconditionality, high costs leading to higher tax rates is probably a major concern. To move people beyond instant rejection of BI on taxation grounds, all ideas about how to finance a BI should be examined. What evidence is available? What assumptions are being made? What trade-offs could be anticipated?

• *What are the positive benefits we could expect from a Canadian BI?*

Jordan (1998:174-76) suggests six benefits of a BI that can recommend it to most people. A discussion of BI for Canada might conclude with a consideration of the extent to which these benefits fulfill the goals and values of Canadians, and of how such benefits might best be assured.

1. *BI is an employment-friendly system.* BI would be much less of a disincentive to seeking employment than either means-tested income support or any other system that withdraws benefits as earnings rise.
2. *A savings-friendly system.* Because BI is not means-tested, it would encourage savings, even by small savers, who could accumulate private property without fear of losing the BI.
3. *Equality of opportunity.* Because BI is provided to all citizens, it promotes equality of opportunity to the extent that such equality is possible. (Especially important in this regard is the necessary context of any BI program: societal investment in people's access to affordable housing, and quality education, health care and child care.)
4. *Targeting those in genuine need.* While they would always have more income than if they had not taken on paid work, people who enter the labour market and earn income above the BI level would pay progressively higher taxes as their incomes rose (as is now the case), as would those who have additional income from non-work sources. So the BI would directly benefit those with the lowest incomes, and would do so without the stigma attached to means tests or other special take-up conditions.

The final two benefits, Jordan believes, would be especially appealing to the well-off.

1. *Slowing down the pace of change.* By damping down competition from women, the young, and the unemployed for the "best" jobs (those held by insiders), BI could delay the impact of globalization on the privileged by offering them "a principle of justice through which they could compensate outsiders for their disadvantages, and still retain some advantages of their own, on the grounds that this would benefit all, by conserving the value of the human capital of the nation state" (Jordan 1998:176).
2. *Minimizing wasteful use of resources and rising social costs.* By offering people support if they choose or are forced to opt out of the

labour market from time to time (a pattern in any case enshrined in the demand for a flexible workforce), a BI lessens the pressure to use resources wastefully or unnecessarily simply to create jobs. As well, a BI would mean significantly reduced costs for welfare-regime staff to screen, scrutinize, advise and discipline targeted aid recipients. And, perhaps most important, a BI would arguably provide a basis on which crimes by the poor against the rich could be decreased and prison expenditures reduced.

ADDITIONAL READINGS

Excerpted from

THE POST-CORPORATE WORLD

By David Korten

> Everyone has the right to a standard of living adequate
> for the health and well-being of himself and of his family,
> including food, clothing, housing, and medical care and
> necessary social services, and the right to security in the
> event of unemployment, sickness, disability, widowhood,
> old age, or other lack of livelihood in circumstances
> beyond his control.
> — Article 25, *Universal Declaration of Human
> Rights of the United Nations*

*E*NGLISH PHILOSOPHER JOHN LOCKE is well known for the moral
defense of private property rights he articulated in *The Second Treatise
of Government,* published in 1689. The defense centres on the
argument that property rights secure the right of persons to a means of
living created by their own labour.

Locke's argument was built on three premises. First, "God gave the
world to men in common."[1] Second, "Men, being once born, have a
right to their preservation, and consequently to meat and drink, and
such other things as nature affords for their subsistence."[2] And third,
"Every man has a property in his own person. This nobody has any
right to but himself. The labour of his body, and the work of his hands,
we may say, are properly his."[3]

Building from these three premises, Locke concluded that "As much
land as a man tills, plants, improves, cultivates, and can use the
product of, so much is his property. He by his labour does, as it were,
enclose it from the common."[4]

Anticipating the criticism that one man's appropriation of a property might thereby deprive another of a means of living, Locke offered the following counterargument:

> Nor was this appropriation of any parcel of land, by improving it, any prejudice to any other man, since there was still enough—and as good—left; and more than the yet unprovided could use. So that, in effect, there was never the less left for others because of this enclosure for himself. For he that leaves as much as another can make use of, does as good as take nothing at all.[5]

By this logic, the right to private property is derived from the right to a means of living. The amount of the property to which one person may rightfully claim exclusive rights is limited to the amount required to produce a basic livelihood by his or her own hand and by the amount of like property available to others.

Locke then moved from the situation of pure agrarian subsistence to that of a society in which monetized exchange and industrial production had become commonplace and there was need to provide for an accumulation of capital, especially in the form of factories and equipment, beyond subsistence needs. Here he sought to rationalize the concentration of property ownership by the assumption that property rights in a monetized economy are most likely to be accumulated by clever and industrious persons who seek to realize the full productive potential of their assets. Such accumulation therefore maximizes the total wealth of society without harm to anyone and improves the well-being of all.[6] It seems, on the face of it, a sensible argument—at least until we see how it plays out in our present setting to become a defense of inequality and exclusion.

Present-day economists of the capitalist persuasion use an argument nearly identical to that of Locke to defend virtually unlimited capital concentration and inequality. In the contemporary version, the wealthy provide the investment capital that fuels economic growth to increase the total wealth of society to the benefit of all and with harm to no one. Note that the validity of the argument rests on three critical assumptions:

- The accumulated capital of the wealthy is invested in productive activity that increases useful output and thereby the total wealth of the society.
- Natural capital remains abundant relative to need so that one person's increased use of land and other resources does not deprive another of like opportunity.
- The benefits of increased useful output are widely shared.

Unfortunately, as we have seen in previous chapters, none of these assumptions currently holds up. The capital being accumulated by the rich is primarily financial and it is used to finance speculative and extractive investments that destroy living capital and future productive capacity. Natural wealth has become scarce relative to need, and its monopolization by the wealthy is actively displacing the poor and depriving them of a means of living. Finally, the benefits of economic growth are going primarily to the top one percent of the world population, while 80 percent suffer stagnation or absolute decline.

Property rights now support three dynamics that ultimately deprive the economically weak of any means of living whatever. They are used to exclude the poor from the land on which they might grow their own subsistence by corporations and wealthy individuals who claim land far beyond their own need for their exclusive use. They are used to eliminate and downgrade as many jobs as possible in a global economy of constantly shifting fortunes and high unemployment. They are used to justify sharp reductions in public services and safety nets on the grounds that taxing the capital-owning classes to provide services and safety nets for the poor amounts to a confiscation of their property to maintain the indolent.

Property rights continue to have an appropriate moral legitimacy when used to secure the right of all individuals as stakeholders in the assets on which they depend to produce a reasonable living for themselves and their families. They lack moral legitimacy, however, when used by those who have more than they need to exclude others from access to a basic means of living or to absolve themselves of responsibility for equitably sharing and stewarding the resources that are the common heritage of all who were born to life on this planet.

Excerpted from

THE BRIEF REIGN OF THE KNOWLEDGE WORKER

By Kit Sims Taylor

*T*HE RELATIONSHIP BETWEEN THE SUPPLY of knowledge labor and the supply of knowledge products is the productivity of knowledge workers, or how much the average knowledge worker produces in an hour. If productivity increases rapidly, it means that the same number of workers working the same number of hours can produce significantly more than they could before. Or, a smaller number of workers could produce the same amount that was produced before. The diversity and non-comparability of the goods and services produced by knowledge workers makes productivity difficult to measure with any accuracy—we can't reduce their output to some measurable standard like tons of steel produced per day—but the concepts of productivity and productivity growth are important nonetheless.

This brings us to the key question of this paper: Is it likely that the effective supply of knowledge work will grow faster than the demand for knowledge products? In the past this has occurred with both agriculture and manufacturing. As the productivity of farmers and farm workers grew faster than the demand for agricultural products, the number of farmers and farm workers had to fall. When the productivity of manufacturing workers grew faster than our demand for manufactured products, the number of manufacturing workers necessarily shrunk. But there are two important differences. Employment in agriculture fell as employment in manufacturing was growing; employment in manufacturing fell as employment in the service sector was growing. And in both agriculture and manufacturing the slow pace of change made it easier for the growing sector to absorb the labor that was being cast out of the shrinking sector. The pace of technological change is much faster now. And there is no apparent sector that can absorb the labor that the knowledge sector casts off or the labor cast off by other sectors that the knowledge sector fails to absorb. When we finally get around to asking "What comes after knowledge work?" we have to admit that there is no answer.

What Do Knowledge Workers Do?

As knowledge workers, we like to think that most of our work involves the creation of new knowledge—of knowledge that would not exist without our mental efforts. Unfortunately, this is actually a fairly small part of our work. When we examine the work pattern of knowledge workers, we find six more or less distinct types of work:

1. Routine work that is hard to separate from knowledge work. Formatting an article, for example, is work that might be done by a typist, but would be done by the knowledge worker when that takes less time than preparing the document and formatting instructions for the typist.
2. Networking, promoting, socializing.
3. Finding the data needed to produce the knowledge.
4. Creating what others have probably already created when this would take less time than to search, find, and appropriate what has been produced by others.
5. Truly original knowledge work—creating what has not been created before.
6. Communicating what has been produced or learned.

The most important distinction is the difference between "4" and "5." We may spend much of our time creating knowledge that is new to us, but is the same or similar to "products" that have been created by other knowledge workers. The fate of most knowledge workers is a worklife in which we are constantly reinventing the exam question, the flood insurance clause, the advertising copy for a sweater ad—producing goods and services that are new to us but not new to the greater society. Such work may well be pleasant and fulfilling. The knowledge worker is indeed engaged in the creation of knowledge. But the knowledge worker is only being paid for it because creating knowledge that exists elsewhere is presently cheaper than finding it.

[. . .]

The Internet and other information technologies have already had a significant impact on knowledge work, even though some of these technologies are still in their infancy. In the near future we can expect information technology to have an even greater impact on all of the aspects of knowledge work that were identified above:

1. Routine work that is hard to separate from knowledge work: The

stand-alone computer has already had a major impact on routine work, but the employment shrinking effects have fallen more on clerical workers than on knowledge workers. This trend will continue as we network more of our computer activities. For example, rather than print out something that needs to be reproduced, then give it to an office worker who—in turn—fills out a form and sends it to the campus copy center, instructors at my college now fill out a form on screen and send documents directly to the copy center over our LAN. Perhaps we only eliminate two minutes of the instructor's time and four minutes of the clerk's time for each document, but it adds up to substantial labor reduction.

2. Networking, promoting, socializing: Email, chat rooms and electronic white boards are presently eliminating a lot of travel and waiting from our networking. As this technology becomes easier to use, and as we become more comfortable with it, more face-to-face communication will be replaced with electronic contact. Many knowledge workers may not like it, but when the institutions that employ us are convinced that electronic connections will do the job, we will find our travel and conference budgets slashed.

3. Finding the data needed to produce the knowledge: The Net has already had a major impact on this aspect of our work. When we consider that as recently as five years ago most of us hadn't yet begun to use the Internet, the potential for the next five years seems almost unlimited. The Internet is already beginning to replace the law library. It will increasingly be used for medical diagnoses, journalism, engineering, and practically every other professional activity.

4. Creating what others have probably already created: This aspect of knowledge work will practically disappear. It will become a form of data gathering or knowledge mining rather than knowledge creation. Whirlpool now puts the engineering details of the many components used in its appliances on its Intranet. "In this way an engineer in Brazil who wants a specific aspect for a new refrigerator can look up the website and borrow an idea that has already been invented for a product in the US or Europe," one of their executives noted. Whirlpool expects to increase productivity of its product designers by 30 percent. For many knowledge workers, creating what others have already created is the major portion of our work. It is also the aspect of our work that will be most impacted by information technology trends.

5. Truly original knowledge work—creating what has not been created

before: Information technology products such as spreadsheets make it much easier—and faster—to test our concepts. Future gains here may be limited, but the unfortunate reality is that this is a small proportion of our work time.

6. Communicating what has been produced or learned: The Internet is emerging as a universal communication medium. As voice and video become easier to integrate with text and graphics, the process of communicating knowledge will meld into the process of creating it.

Who Gets the Income?

For his final New York Times column, Peter Passell chose the topic of the distribution of income. "For the last quarter century," he wrote—referring to the U.S. economy—"virtually all the bounty of growth has gone to the educated, enterprising and already-affluent." We can identify two major forces—both moving in the same direction—that operated to skew the distribution of income. One was the increase in real interest rates, which benefitted the owners of money. Interest made up 9.2 percent of personal income in 1973 and 13.3 percent by 1995. The share of total income earned as wages, salaries and fringe benefits fell from 74.3 percent to 71.5 percent over the same period. The other was the decline in the value of routine labor relative to the value of college-educated labor. In 1979 the median male college graduate earned 42 percent more than his high school graduate counterpart; by 1998 his college education premium had risen to 89 percent.

Another—less expected—factor in increasing earnings inequality has been growing inequality of earnings within occupations. This trend has been particularly pronounced in the white collar professions. One of the causes of this intra-occupation skewing is the proliferating computerization of business. According to Robert H. Frank and Philip J. Cook in The Winner-Take-All Society, the ability of computerized production processes to gather data as well as produce goods increases the leverage of the most able participants: "No matter what new organizational forms ultimately emerge, the cumulative effect of these changes will be to increase still further the leverage of the economy's most able performers."

Frank and Cook's observations were made in 1995, just as many knowledge workers were taking our first tentative clicks into the Internet. The technological trends noted earlier in this paper can only serve to accelerate these earnings trends. We will not only have superstar CEOs and superstar attorneys, but superstar fire-insurance-policy authors and superstar egg-marketing experts whose Web-distributed services will bring them greater earnings while curtailing opportunities for others in those fields.

Whenever productivity increases someone gains, but it is not always the worker. Labor market conditions—notably the unemployment rate, the degree of competition among firms, and institutional factors such as the strength of government—will all affect the distribution of the gains from increased productivity. With sufficient competition productivity gains may be spread throughout the society via lower prices. With low unemployment rates and/or strong unions they will be spread via higher wages. Government might capture the gains through taxation and spread them to society via spending on education or health care. If unemployment is high, unions are weak, firms face little competition, and government lacks the ability to increase taxes, productivity gains will accrue to the firms' managers as higher salaries and to the firms' owners as higher profits. . . .

If the high productivity growth stemming from the new information technologies leads to even moderate technological unemployment, it is likely that the gains will be captured by a few superstars, a handful of top managers, and the owners of the firms. The same network effects that make a product more valuable to us when others use it as well (such as email systems and computer operating systems) have the effect of reducing competition. And the very technologies that make distance irrelevant give many firms a global choice of locations which weakens the power of government. . . .

An increasing concentration of income and wealth is not only an unfortunate development in terms of equity, but will also tend to slow economic growth. People of average income spend most of it on consumer goods; people with very high incomes will invest a large part of it. If consumption growth slows, there will be fewer investment opportunities. If our average consumer cannot afford gobs of the new products that include microchips, Motorola, Intel and IBM are not going to invest in new production facilities.

[. . .]

The Institutional Challenge

Our socioeconomic system faces both an opportunity and a challenge. The opportunity is the possibility of an abundant flow of goods and services with very little work—in the traditional sense—on our part. The truly creative activities that cannot be automated will be challenging and fulfilling—cleaning up the environmental damage from the industrial era; finding ways to extend life and health; space exploration; writing operas; etc. . . .

The challenge lies in redesigning our economic institutions to break the link between production and income. This link has served capitalism well for the last two to three centuries. We applied our labor, our land, and/or our capital to the production process. In return we earned wages, rent, or profits. These earnings supported our demand for goods and services. Our demand, in turn, allowed the production process to continue. As we applied more capital and knowledge to the production process, the productivity of our labor increased. When firms were small, competition among them assured that increasing productivity led to lower prices. When this occurred with basic goods such as food, clothing or transportation, the lower prices meant an improved standard of living for most members of society. When unemployment was low, the competition for workers assured that increasing productivity supported higher wages, again leading to an improved standard of living for many.

The rising real wages—whether they came from falling prices or an increase in money wages—fed demand. With demand increasing, higher productivity was used to boost output, not to reduce overall employment. And rising wages plus growing demand also pushed firms into finding more ways to increase productivity—usually by introducing new equipment a rapid rate. We enjoyed the effects of a virtuous circle of growth in productivity, wages, and demand.

Growth was not always smooth. There were periods in which the linkages from production to income to demand and back to production failed us. When the failure was serious enough and long enough it led to major institutional changes. During the last quarter of the 19th century decreases in the prices of basic goods and services such as steel and shipping were sufficiently steep to force waves of bankruptcies and bring new investment to a halt. Oligopoly and antitrust laws were among the new institutions that were subsequently created—allowing firms once again to expand with some hope of profits but with legal constraints on their power.

A more severe breakdown of the basic linkages of capitalism occurred in the 1930s. During the 1920s productivity in manufacturing had increased rapidly, but manufacturing wages had not. Out of the Great Depression came a much larger government role in influencing the distribution of income. In the United States this included laws facilitating the formation of industrial unions, social security, a minimum wage, minimum agricultural prices, and numerous other interventions. John Maynard Keynes provided a theoretical justification for this new form of capitalism in which government was responsible for maintaining sufficient levels of income and demand to keep unemployment low and growth rates high.

Unfortunately, a larger government role in the distribution of income is a rather unpopular idea at present. Even in countries whose citizenry expect and endorse a major government role in income distribution—France and the Scandinavian countries, for example—the ability of firms to leave and take jobs with them has limited the effective scope of government action. Yet the leaps in productivity inherent in the new information technologies cannot be realized without markets for the oceans of knowledge-based goods and services that we will soon be capable of producing. If we leave the distribution of income primarily to market institutions, the demand for knowledge products cannot keep up with the effective supply of knowledge products. It would be far better to begin a dialogue now on the economic institutions that we will need in the near future rather than wait—as we have done in the past—for a depression or other economic calamity to force institutional change upon us. The last depression brought us the New Deal programs and Keynesian economics that helped fuel consumer demand in the post-WWII economy; but it also brought us the deadly detour of fascism.

What comes after knowledge work? The choice is ours. If we fail to adapt our economic institutions to accommodate the extremely high productivity that will become possible, we may well face constant depression combined with a distribution of income that will be more extreme than we find today in countries such as Brazil and Mexico. Or we can enjoy lives without toil; lives in which we can take an abundance of goods and services for granted; lives without work as we know it today; lives filled with creative and fulfilling activities.

THE DANCE OF THE DEFICIT AND THE REAL WORLD OF WEALTH: RETHINKING ECONOMIC MANAGEMENT FOR SOCIAL PURPOSE

By Rod Dobell

*I*N THIS CHAPTER, we survey briefly the argument that a welfare system founded substantially on a central government commitment to full employment is no longer plausible and conclude, with others, that the evidence is persuasive. Something better is needed as a framework for social policy. Fifty years after the last major reformulation of the welfare system and two hundred years after the main principles of our present market economy were articulated and the sources of national wealth (as seen at that time) documented, it is time to rethink what an appropriate social or institutional response might be to the challenges of the economic world as we now understand it.

The key point is that the forms of wealth or capital central to the knowledge-based, innovation-driven service economy and global information society in which we now live go far beyond raw labour and financial or physical capital: they include skills, knowledge, information and intellectual property; institutional, social and cultural capital;[1] and ecological or natural capital. The creation of wealth in fact rests fundamentally on the increase of social and natural capital. These are the crucial investments our society must make in the current and coming decades. Yet our commercial institutions and our accounting systems lead us astray: we count as "unproductive"—as contributing to deficits—almost all the investments we make for these purposes.

The evidence is now conclusive that we must view the economy more broadly than does conventional economic analysis. Economic mechanisms must be seen as set within the structure of social institutions (including family, household, voluntary sector and civil society generally) within which much of the work of society is conducted. This work is not in the formal economy—it is not paid for in any fashion that brings it into market transactions or economic accounts. Nonetheless, recognition of this broader concept of work extends economic decisions into a public or social sphere and underlines the importance to economic performance of relationships and investment decisions in this realm. The "economically inactive" should not continue to be "policy-irrelevant."

It is also becoming both clear and widely accepted that the ultimate foundation for economic performance is established by the natural systems of the biosphere. To understand economic performance and assure a competitive economy we must extend economic reasoning to consider the ecological systems and underlying resources on which all material well-being is finally based.[2]

In particular, our concept of social support should be based on a social contract, not social insurance. The creation of a social contract is not an act of charity born of compassion, but a necessary investment in a cohesive society and a market economy that can support internationally competitive enterprises. It is thus an investment born of enlightened self-interest for the community as a whole. The social contract we envisage assures a basic income paid to all citizens for two reasons: first, as participants in productive social networks and active contributors to social wealth creation; and, second, as owners of the social capital, represented by social networks and community knowledge, and of the scarce natural capital, represented by the ecological commons, which together form the foundation for market activity. The affordability of the social contract emerges partly from essential repricing of the services of those resources, partly as a result of the revised conceptual framework that will result from better bookkeeping and partly as a recognition that we who are comfortable are going to have to pay something for an essential social commitment that goes beyond an insistence on individual responsibility for individual well-being.

Three ground swells in the social and economic world dramatically alter the context in which welfare provisions must operate: labour market restructuring; our approach to ecological carrying capacity; and the emergence of a networked, increasingly global, civil society. In light of these transformations, a reorientation of social policy toward sharing the costs of economic adaptation and pooling the risks of adjustment in an innovation-driven society seems essential. Specifically, this chapter argues for a guaranteed annual income, or basic income.[3]

A brief review of the evidence suggests that some integrated tax-transfer scheme offering a reasonable assured minimum income to all citizens is feasible and that it is possible to finance the necessary outlays—in part by shifting some of the present tax burden from income to consumption through the repricing of ecological resources. The implied balance of responsibilities amongst governments and other organizations, relying largely on markets but increasingly on voluntary organizations and quasi-market mechanisms, seems plausible; the relationship is consistent with what we need to do in any case in pursuit of ecological and social sustainability. Perhaps the problems are now sufficiently severe and the urgency sufficiently widely recognized to generate the political will to overcome the predictable resistance of the organizations—academic, professional, bureaucratic and union— that will strive mightily to protect privileged positions against any obligation to share in the adjustment costs of an innovative, adaptive and open economy.

None of this is new, but it seems we still have a very long way to go in facing up to the economic consequences of technological developments and maturing social movements.

New World, New Circumstances
Economic Change and Labour Market Restructuring

The story of our changing economy—centred on processes of technological change; processes for the diffusion of ideas, knowledge and innovation; and the impacts of such changes on skill requirements—has been rehearsed in many places. Lipsey[4] offers a wide-ranging account of the forces underlying contemporary economic transformations. Osberg, Wolfe and Baumol[5] explore some implications for labour markets. Evidence is growing that the move toward a knowledge-based economy is increasing labour market polarization.[6] In addition, the degree of inequality in the distribution of primary incomes or overall earnings is increasing and is only partly offset by transfers.[7] The problems of long-term unemployment associated with older workers and unskilled younger workers seems likely to grow and to aggravate these trends.

As early as 1930, Keynes[8] anticipated unemployment as the result of the immense productivity increases caused by technological developments. Yet British, US and Canadian policy papers and legislation in the mid-1940s affirmed that Western governments believed that it was their responsibility to assure full employment in the postwar world.[9] In 1994, after nearly 50 years of bruising social and economic change, the Organization for Economic Cooperation and Development (OECD) takes a somewhat less presumptuous view and advises that there is no single recipe for full employment, but rather a menu of measures that can help move OECD economies towards higher employment with good jobs.[10] It is the OECD's contention that high unemployment is the direct result of the inability of economies and societies to adapt to rapid change.

One of the difficulties for most modern economies is that their insurance-based models of social security, which assume that something close to full employment normally prevails, actually hinder the adaptation to change that is so desperately needed for economic and social survival in a post-industrial world. The current concept of social insurance assumes steady economic growth and assured prospects for full employment in the formal labour force. It functions best in a society where there are numerous and relatively prosperous employed earners, where income inadequacies arise primarily from short-term interruption to earnings and where entitlement is related to previous contributions and contingency rather than income. The percentage of unemployed people receiving social insurance in most OECD countries has decreased sharply since the 1960s, a result directly attributable to contingencies not recognized by the traditional social insurance model. These include long-term unemployment, sustained youth unemployment, the growth of non-standard employment and the tightening of contribution requirements—attributable in large measure to the social learning on the part of both employees and employers that enables the individual production costs associated with fluctuating demand for labour to be shifted to the collective pool. Furthermore, with the growth of employer-provided benefits and pensions, as well as private income among the elderly, the original contingencies of old age, illness, death of the breadwinner and unemployment are no longer automatic determinants of need.

It is estimated that 35 million people are unemployed in OECD countries and that another 15 million have either given up looking for work or have unwillingly accepted part-time work.[11] The link between work and wages as the basic mode of income distribution is clearly inadequate for most modern economies. People continue to define their social role primarily in terms of participation in production and to derive substantial self-esteem and meaning from work. But the range of productive work far exceeds the range of employment, and a new social contract must recognize a broader concept of contribution: it must include income from both formal and informal work[12] and benefits that are not contingent solely upon participation in the formal labour market.[13]

In a prescient analysis of the early 1980s, Rotstein[14] makes a case for government policies that support the informal economy. He argues that the three primary forms of economic activity—reciprocity, redistribution and market exchange—all take place in the informal economy. To the extent that redistribution in the formal economy has been taken over by the state and that the current welfare state is only viable within the context of stable, decently paid jobs, Rotstein questions our dependence on market networks to the exclusion of other forms of exchange: "It is precisely the ability of informal networks to identify and address new social and economic needs . . . that makes possible the creation of new circuits of production and consumption. These networks coexist with and feed into the formal market. The informal economy can thus serve as the source of a series of potential new economic activities upon which policymakers can draw to supplement and expand the number of registered and wage-remunerated employment opportunities." It is also worth noting that it is in the activities of this "third sector" that the comparative advantage of humans over machines in dealing with variety and situational complexity is likely to have its greatest impact in increased employment.[15]

Sustainability and the Full-World Economy

The publication of the World Conservation Strategy[16] in 1980 introduced sustainability as a key feature in public policy making. Work in environmental economics has since argued for much broader acceptance of methods to integrate environmental considerations into economic decisions by pricing resources and ecological services more appropriately. But this argument, although it represents important progress, still has the basic relationships backwards. Ecological economics, by contrast, integrates economic decisions within broader recognition of social institutions and sets all those within the framework of the biosphere, the network of natural dynamics that forms the life-support system for humanity.

The failures of price systems, financial accounting systems and systems of national accounts to capture essential features of transactions involving natural capital or environmental amenities are widely recognized.[17] Also recognized is the necessity of correcting flawed markets with fiscal instruments like "green taxes," or creating new markets for trading in new property rights, or implementing "polluter-pay principles" of the sort advocated by the OECD since the early 1970s. Such measures are now seen as essential to correct otherwise misleading market signals and misinformed economic decisions.[18] Kennedy[19] emphasizes the importance of public assets in attempts to achieve real reform in income security. Beyond the simple correction of market calculations and social performance indicators, more profound restructuring of social decision-making is occurring with the attempt to find consultative procedures and processes of shared decision-making designed to assure adequate preservation and renewal of scarce natural capital.[20]

What these developments mean for public policy is that, along with investment in social infrastructure to assure opportunities for individual participation in useful social roles, public investment activity designed to protect or restore the foundation of natural capital on which the economy rests is also a critical infrastructure investment—a key investment in a productive resource base. The consequence, which has perhaps not yet been fully recognized, is that there must be dramatic adaptation of markets and production structures to more informed recognition of these costs through the widespread introduction of user charges and "green taxes." While these attempts at repricing are designed primarily to improve market information, they do offer new revenue sources as well. These revenues could be earmarked to employ large numbers of people in the work of conservation, preservation and adaptation of the economy to the massive structural changes that must follow when the repricing and revaluation necessary in the pursuit of sustainable development is more properly reflected throughout the price system and market mechanisms generally.

The transition to a "full" world, one that is feeling the pressure on limits to carrying capacity, reflects the scale problems arising from both global population growth, primarily in the South, and intensive consumption and production activity, primarily in the North. As natural capital becomes scarce, it must be priced and rationed in production; its value must be accounted for in wealth estimates and national accounts, and the incomes generated by its use must flow to its owners. The owners of these resources are the citizens of the nation, who share in the returns to the resource as a matter of right, not as a matter of redistribution. This profound transformation in pricing mechanisms and production structures, necessary when the role of natural capital is recognized, is one factor leading to a radical revision of the conceptual bases underlying arguments for an assured minimum income.

Concepts of wealth creation and the sort of work that represents wealth creation thus have to be substantially broadened. Conservation corps, for example, or habitat improvement activities, which might never pass a standard test of commercial viability to the satisfaction of local bankers, nevertheless have to be recognized as wealth-creating. High rates of return on forest ventures that rest on practices that destroy salmon habitat and erode forest lands, or profitable fishing ventures harnessing technologies that strip the seabed but use only minuscule proportions of a massive by-catch, must, on the other hand, be seen as wealth-destroying. With this broader notion of wealth creation, we can see participation in the economy and contribution to society in a wide range of activities that increase the sustainability and growth of ecological, human and social capital.

Re-emergence of Civil Society: Home Realm of the New Social Capital

Liberal democracy has always required the existence of a third realm, independent of the market and state, to act on behalf of community and societal interests. Historically, this third realm of civil society has not been treated as a system because of its lack of a strong, unique form of organization equivalent to the hierarchical institutions of government or the competitive markets of the economy. However, information technologies and related innovations in management and administration are enabling the network form of organization to gain strength.

In a provocative recent paper, Ronfeldt and Thorup[21] argue that the advent of information technologies has led to the erosion of hierarchy, diffusion of power, blurring of boundaries and opening up of closed systems, all of which combine to challenge the supremacy and efficiency of both government institutions and atomized markets, while at the same time increasing the power and effectiveness of informal social and economic networks. The information revolution is making it possible for many previously small, weak and isolated actors to communicate, consult and co-ordinate with one another as never before. This trend heralds the transformation of society into a more complex, interconnected structure—a multiorganizational network—resulting in a new balance of power among the state, market and civil society. This new balance will force greater attention to the importance of non-market activity and non-profit institutions and will have significant impact on the way economic decisions are made.[22]

Some implications for policy makers are clear. First, they can expect an explosive growth of activity in the realm of civil society across North America, with opportunities for co-operation, competition and conflict in and among the state, market and civil society. Second, they can expect an increase in public and citizen diplomacy with the need to rethink and reorganize the relationship between government and civil society at all levels. And finally, the integration of civil societies as well as markets will require governments to develop new criteria for successful international relations, embedding trade and commercial relations more explicitly within international commitments to environmental and social principles.

More concretely, however, these developments underline the importance of the cultural or social capital within which productive activity is organized. The development of social networks, and the rules and understandings on which they operate, are critical to production.[23] This social wealth has measurable economic value. The skills and knowledge that are widely acknowledged as key to future prosperity are exercised within the framework of this institutional capital or social infrastructure. It is this collective institutional capital—the capacity to build and effectively use individual skills and knowledge—that forms the basis of the wealth of nations or regions. And it is this social or cultural capital that determines whether the critical interface of our human activities with our natural home—the biosphere—will be effectively managed.[24]

Rethinking Social Policy: The New Social Contract

A high degree of social consensus will be needed to move forward with the changes made necessary by rapid technological change and globalization. Some people will have particular difficulty making these changes. Yet by excluding the people slower to adapt or precluded by circumstances from doing so, mainstream society risks creating social tensions that could carry a high human and economic cost for all. Refusal to share broadly the costs of adjustment forces persistent recourse to all the work rules and rigidities that impede necessary adaptation. By refusing to address human security, we force an obsolete clinging to job security throughout an economy that should be more flexible.

A social contract provides security—individual and collective—from the risks of economic change and global competition. The pooling of risks through social insurance, social assistance or regional adjustment is a natural response of any community observing the problems that individuals face in adapting to changing circumstances. This bargain entails accepting the need for social investment in human capital formation, in institution building and in restoration and preservation of renewable resources as a legitimate charge on the public purse. In the new economy, public support for services such as education, health and social welfare—and, indeed, provisions for career development and job transition—are not forms of social policy representing non-productive consumption, but are investments in human capital, which contribute directly and significantly to economic growth, development and productivity. They generate their own tangible economic returns in the future. They should no more be treated as a burden on future generations than should corporate borrowing for new facilities and equipment.

The spectre of declining real incomes in a highly indebted North America demands new strategies and mechanisms for maintaining social cohesion. The polarization of income distribution also demands other mechanisms to bridge the enclaves created by sustained high unemployment and the "good jobs, bad jobs" phenomenon. In an era of economic quick fixes and short-term solutions to dogged social problems, the prolonged adjustment period required to move us onto a new track of ecologically and socially sustainable development also necessitates an openness and responsiveness to market signals that can only be achieved by pooling the risks and shocks of an uncertain world through new mechanisms of income redistribution. The need for new mechanisms, in turn, forces us to re-examine the nature of participation in the family, neighbourhood, school, workplace, province or region, nation and global community. When productivity is more broadly defined in both the formal and informal economies, it can be seen that a social role and a productive place in the economy can be found through paid employment, self-employment, education and training, voluntary work, community development or environmental conservation.

And finally, we need to examine distributional issues arising around questions of access to the infrastructure and media of the information society. Economic or educational barriers to use of communications technologies, databases and network services not only can exacerbate problems of income distribution, but also will raise even more fundamental issues of democratic participation and civic roles. The challenge is to develop a policy framework within which all of these issues can be seen as part of the whole rather than as separate sectoral concerns, and through which we can examine the impact of a necessary repricing and restructuring of market activities in the direction of social cohesion and ecological sustainability.

For this, the social contract must reflect the features enunciated 50 years ago by Rhys Williams: "The State would acknowledge the duty to maintain individuals and their children at all times, and to ensure for them the necessities of a healthy life. Individuals, in their turn, would acknowledge it to be their duty to devote their best efforts to the production of the wealth whereby alone the welfare of the community can be maintained."[25] The social contract entails personal obligation and commitment, a responsibility to participate and contribute in an evolving economy that has forfeited much of its apparatus of job security. But it does so on the basis of a social commitment to a minimum participation income reflecting that contribution and the inherent claims of all Canadians to a share of the returns of the social network and ecological commons that make up Canada.[26]

Rethinking the Mechanics of Distribution: The Candidate Scheme

The idea endorsed here is essentially the guaranteed income with a simple tax (GI/ST) developed by Wolfson.[27] Similar principles are found in the basic income guarantee with partial integration of the tax and transfer system (BI 2000) developed by Parker,[28] and are reflected also in the concept of participation income discussed by Atkinson.[29] They can be found in the support-supplementation proposals of the Federal—Provincial Social Security Review of the early 1970s, and in the universal income security program (UISP) proposed by the Macdonald Commission.

The fiscally neutral GI/ST proposed by Wolfson harmonizes the personal income tax and transfer systems while simplifying and consolidating existing programs, improving incentives and providing more support to the working poor. It starts from the simple idea of combining a guaranteed income with a flat tax embodying a constant marginal tax rate. If a flat tax is tied to an initial income guarantee, the result is a progressive structure in which average rates of tax increase with income, even though marginal tax rates are constant.

A guaranteed annual income already exists in piecemeal form for the elderly and families with children through Old Age Security, the Guaranteed Income Supplement and a child tax benefit. The recombination of these into one program serves as the basis of the guaranteed income portion of the GI/ST. The child tax benefit, Guaranteed Income Supplement, Canada Assistance Plan, married and equivalent-to-married exemptions, basic personal exemption and age exemption as well as pension, employment and investment deductions would all be abolished—rolled into a basic income paid to all individuals without means testing or a formal work requirement.

The program could be further enriched by incorporating existing unemployment insurance provisions as well. A UI scheme addressed to income continuity for people with generally secure opportunities in the formal labour market might be established on private, rather than social, insurance principles, with any public resources thereby freed flowing to the higher-priority basic minimum income.

In place of the abolished programs and tax provisions, a set of basic federal income guarantees would function as an income supplementation tier. The federal government would thus assume responsibility for the working poor and provide a nationally uniform minimum income for all Canadians. Provinces would then have full responsibility for providing the top-up income support to the poorest; they could tailor this income support according to region-specific factors in ways that are perhaps inappropriate for the federal government.

To address the issue of progressivity, the GI/ST incorporates a two-step tax rate structure, rather than the completely flat tax described above. One single basic federal rate of tax, applied to net income, would replace all existing income tax brackets. A surtax on income above a certain threshold would then be levied on total income. With no personal exemptions, tax would start on the first dollar of net income. The federal—provincial tax collection agreements would be retained, but provincial tax rates as a percentage of the new federal basic tax (including the surtax) would be reduced to reflect the resulting broader tax base. (It should be noted that the simplicity and attendant efficiencies of the flat tax rate of the GI/ST would be lost if provinces were to impose their own complicated rate structures.)

In terms of delivery and responsiveness, the GI/ST lends itself to the use of the source withholding system for income tax because the integrated basic flat rate of tax applies over the entire income spectrum and uses the individual as the taxpaying or beneficiary unit. As income testing could be substantially integrated into the source withholding system, the issue of universality vs. selectivity becomes considerably less relevant. A more relevant issue is whether spouses who stay at home to care for children and elders should receive their own and their dependents' guarantees in full, or whether these should be netted against the working spouses' income tax liabilities.

With modest amendment to the basic design, the GI/ST could be targeted more specifically toward redistribution within the income spectrum, and also more targeted in its redistribution within and among family groups. But, as emphasized below, the inevitability of some redistribution must be faced. Under the GI/ST design explored by Wolfson in 1986,[30] just under half of all families would experience net declines in disposable income.

Wolfson contends that the conceptual changes involved in the GI/ST are more daunting than the practical changes in delivery systems. At the federal level, there would no longer be any difference between income transfers and income taxes; both would be part of the same integrated system whose primary objective is redistribution. A possible obstacle, however, might be that "bureaucrats involved with the welfare and transfer system are unlikely to recommend substantial simplification to the current system because they would, in effect, be suggesting major disruption in their own [professional] lives."[31] Also, potential beneficiaries of piecemeal redistributive programs will lobby hard for their continuance, and a proliferation of specific policies will typically generate more votes than a systematic overall redistributive system—a political incentive that is not easily ignored. However, the fiscal incentives may yet outweigh the risks. The GI/ST is more elastic with respect to real income growth than the current system. This means that the federal deficit would fall more quickly with GI/ST as the economy moved toward full employment and real incomes grew than it would under the current income security system. (Wolfson also notes that the netting of benefits against taxes owing can have a large impact on total dollar flows and a corresponding effect on the apparent size of the federal government, depending on whether the income guarantees are treated as direct spending programs or refundable tax credits.)

A minimum participation income would cushion the shocks of adjustment to and in the new world economy. It is the logical support to an emerging dual structure within the economy: a competitive, high-productivity, high-income, technology- and capital-intensive sector with a rapid redeployment of labour, co-existing with a publicly financed, labour-intensive service sector that cannot justify comparable wages, especially while operating under conditions of continuing fiscal restraint. A minimum participation income also promises much more efficient labour markets.[32]

It is worth noting that this sort of scheme is not inconsistent with—indeed, it complements well—an approach based on restructuring incentives toward reduced hours of work, particularly in the high-income enclaves of the labour market. The 1994 edition of the *Human Development Report* contains a brief but very positive reference to job-sharing as another avenue to reduced unemployment and improved income distribution.[33] With the broader concept of work and participation advocated here, implementation of this approach would be simplified: it amounts simply to shifting the balance at the margin between contribution in the formal workplace and contribution in civil society or the informal workplace.

The minimum participation income, then, becomes a form of social consensus on fair ground rules for sharing the burden of adjustment costs. But the proposal is not without cost. Even though it might be made fiscally neutral in aggregate, the GI/ST does involve redistribution. The question, then, is whether there exists yet in Canada any appetite for such redistribution or any prospect of the necessary tax changes.[34]

Volumes have been written on all these issues; several have been cited above. Without going into specific features, the simple point of this section is that a reasonable case can be made for the feasibility and effectiveness of an integrated system for delivery of a basic minimum income.

Reality Check: Taxable Capacity and the Race to the Bottom

All the above is well and good as thoughts for the longer term. But there is no denying the urgency of the current fiscal crisis or the simple arithmetic of accumulating debt. We must address our foreign debt as a basic constraint on sovereignty and government policy discretion. We must address our government debt more generally, because interest payments increasingly eat up program space. Addressing these obstacles, particularly the former, undoubtedly entails a considerable period of underspending as a nation—a course on which the federal government has embarked and to which it seems committed. But underspending need not mean underinvestment. Tax and spending changes both should aim at encouraging reduced consumption rather than the abdication of social responsibilities or the loss of social investment.

The threat of capital strike is everywhere. It is said that if we do not produce what the gnomes of the rating agencies like in the way of budgets, essential capital inflows will dry up. If we do not do what corporations would like in the way of taxes, plants will move. This argument may be overdone. Survey data and anecdotal evidence suggest that location decisions are considerably more comprehensive than implied by the capital-strike argument. The location decisions of firms consider the availability and character of skilled labour force. And a cohesive body of skilled people seems more likely to be available if the quality of life is there. Natural capital and social capital are not mobile (though both are exhaustible). The growth of a networked civil society makes it less likely that firms will see advantage in chasing each other in a "race to the bottom," where countries compete to offer the most lax regulatory environment or the most generous tax regime. Indeed, the relative lack of mobility of scarce natural and social capital provides a basis for the reintroduction of theories of comparative advantage, which have been seen to be increasingly irrelevant as a basis for reasoning about social welfare in a world of where human and intellectual capital are mobile, along with financial capital, goods and services.[35]

The notion of "taxable capacity" is a notoriously slippery concept. Colin Clark, a famous precursor of the minimal government school, is credited with what once was thought an iron law of public finance: when government expenditure exceeds 25% of national income, you hit a wall. Clark's conclusion was directed toward the dynamics of price formation: the "wall" was a "general rise in costs and prices."[36] But observers made the leap from the inflation problem to a more general "wall"—taxable capacity—fairly readily.

In company with most other developed economies, we are, of course, considerably beyond that limit by now. Perry[37] gives us—with many careful qualifications—some interpretation of international comparisons using the OECD's annual compilation of revenue statistics.[38] What he reports is that from 1990 to 1992, Canada moved from a ranking of 12th to 11th in the OECD tables showing the ratio of total tax revenues to gross domestic product (GDP) in each country. These comparisons also show that, despite all the talk of killer payroll taxes, Canada relies very much less on this revenue source (as a percentage of GDP) than do other OECD countries. Moreover, in non-tax revenues, including charges for use of natural resources or ecological services, Canada ranked below 10 other OECD countries, including the United States. Despite predictable apprehensions about the distortion of market allocations, such charges are not bad just because they enter production costs—the question is whether they represent real costs. If so, they should be levied (and Canada may have more room for such charges because we have more natural capital at risk).

Thus, it seems that Canadians are not in fact as heavily taxed relative to others as current rhetoric might suggest. Indeed, so far as a general social acceptability of tax burdens in industrialized countries is concerned, Canada occupies a rather traditional position near the centre of the OECD pack. Nevertheless, it is the tax regimes of our particular "competitors," rather than more general comparisons, that set a limit on taxable capacity.[39] In this case, we have to worry about levels of taxation in Japan and the United States, particularly the latter.

Both fall very close to the bottom of the OECD tables. The issue, then, is not general social willingness to pay taxes, but the mobility of capital and labour and the problem of downward harmonization—the convergence of social and environmental policies toward some lowest common denominator. As with this issue in other settings, the response has to be to look at the evidence in context. "Pollution havens," for example, do not suck in all production activity.[40] And even if not valued symmetrically, the greater social wage payable from higher taxes must also be taken into account, as the plaintive laments of Mr. Iaccoca about the unfair competition of Canada's health system attest. Surveys of location decisions suggest at least some evidence that executive locations may reflect quality of social, physical and natural environment, school conditions and other such "non-economic" concerns at least as much as tax rates on personal incomes.

It can be argued that one need not look further than current political action and electoral circumstances to verify that the willingness of the Canadian public to be taxed has reached its limit. But again, as with other conclusions drawn from electoral signals, it is not clear precisely what stimulus is provoking the observed response. There is scattered evidence of greater willingness to pay taxes earmarked for approved purposes, particularly in relation to environmental concerns.[41] For example, "the Environmental Monitor research shows an energy tax, properly explained, would be supported by a majority in all regions of the country, if all resulting revenue was used to reduce air pollution."[42]

With ecological tax reform, the tax base shifts substantially to the resource rents generated by natural capital as economic transactions are linked to their ecological setting.[43] Ecological taxes do not represent the introduction of new revenue instruments for their own sake, but rather the recognition of the need on the part of resource owners, including governments,[44] to price resources and ecological services more realistically to reflect the growing scarcity (and hence growing production value) of natural capital and our increasing concerns about sustainability.

This appeal to improved market functioning is crucial not just from a distributional perspective, but for allocative efficiency as well. The introduction of ecological taxes could finance much local community activity in resource restoration and habitat enhancement, which would be carried out by community conservation corps and similar entities, some possibly outside the existing formal economy. An increase in stumpage rates, water rates or other charges for ecological services is not to be construed as a cause for a taxpayer revolt—it is simply a reflection of decisions by the owners of the resource to price more appropriately services that others wish to purchase for inputs into production.

In reassigning revenue sources (except for "carbon taxes" or other "green" taxes introduced to meet international commitments—for example, on greenhouse gas emissions), the ecological tax revenues would presumably accrue principally to the provinces and be earmarked for ecological and social infrastructure investment and the financing of plans for labour transition and retraining. Integrated sales taxes and the GST could be collected by the provinces with a rebate to the federal government. Income taxes, with perhaps a surtax above a certain income threshold for deficit reduction purposes, would continue to be collected by the federal government. Hawken[45] suggests the political necessity of having every incremental dollar collected from ecological taxes used to reduce income and payroll taxes; others suggest that any such revenues must be allocated to deficit reduction (whatever that financial sleight-of-hand might mean). We remain more optimistic that the use of resource rents to finance the transition out of unsustainable activities and the maintenance of the natural capital base will prove persuasive and acceptable in the longer run.

Still, in the short run, we have a problem. Beneath the insistent beat of the Bay Street drums pounding out the dance of the deficit, another theme can be heard: that there is simply no choice—that we have, even at the level of the nation as a whole, simply no discretion left to continue a tradition of social policy based upon a sense of shared responsibility. Repeatedly we are warned that if we do not mount a sufficiently vigorous assault on the social support system, in which the leisured unemployed are said to be lounging, the hordes of the international financial bureaucracy will no longer wait outside our gates. We will have our social policy made for us.

This sense of impotence at the level of the sovereign state seems in strange contrast to a growing sense of self-sufficiency expressed at the community level as groups increasingly come together to pursue common goals of community economic development and sustainability. It also seems a little premature in a nation like Canada. There is absolutely no doubt that existing structures do need reform and that the deficit problem must be attacked vigorously and effectively. We do have to get debt service obligations down dramatically, simply to avoid a continuing structural budget deficit while program outlays fall far short of tax revenues. But it is still possible to mount this attack on our own terms, in our own way, as Canadians, if we can marshal our resources more consciously.

There is, however, a practical problem. Even if we could agree that much of what is considered government current expenditure would, in a more comprehensive analysis, be recognized as accumulation of productive capital (contributing to the wealth of the nation and properly counted neither as a deficit nor as an intergenerational burden), we are still heavily mortgaged. Our external creditors might not agree with our investments in long-term productivity through human, cultural and natural capital. And as every farmer knows, the name on the bottom of the mortgage has the last word (and frequently a short-term outlook). We lack discretion on fundamental policies and values for the crass but sufficient reason that we owe so much money to outsiders.

Why can we do nothing about this problem? If we are truly facing a national emergency and we find it essential to reduce current levels of debt service, particularly on foreign debt, if we are to have revenues for program outlays, let us consider some emergency measures.

A first and obvious measure will occur to any member of a private club or partnership—a one-time capital levy collected by the federal government, payable over, say, three to five years. The proceeds of this levy would be dedicated to retirement of the federal government's foreign debt as it matures or could be called, with any interim surplus held in trust for repayment as debt matures in the future. Such a measure has the advantage of aiming the big guns directly on the root problem behind the current crisis—the overhanging burden of foreign debt service—by drawing on the assets of the most well-off rather than plodding along with the modest flow of expenditure savings that can be reallocated from annual flows by squeezing the least well-off. In times of crisis, we perhaps should consider recourse to such unusual measures.

Other possibilities spring to mind. In 1995, the 50th anniversary of the end of World War II, entrepreneur Bob Blair and a few other voices were heard suggesting that something like a Canada Social Responsibility Bond, modelled on the Victory Bond, might be able to draw out pools of capital willing to forgo the final margin of optimized financial return in support of a common national cause as important as reducing our foreign debt. We might contemplate withdrawing preferential tax treatment on RRSPS or other pension funds invested in foreign assets, thus strengthening demands for Canadian assets and reducing the need for Canadian governments to borrow abroad. Vallee[46] suggests a much more dramatic and potentially controversial—but also potentially powerful—possibility in switching from a philosophy of preferential treatment for contributions to RRSPS and taxation of withdrawals to one of contributions out of after-tax income and tax-free withdrawals. In the flat-tax world envisaged above, there would be no disadvantage to taxpayers in such a switch—and it opens up the possibility of a retroactive recapturing of the accumulated funds lent by governments to taxpayers through past preferential tax treatment, with substantial favourable impact on government debts and deficits.

Still more fundamentally, recognizing that the pool of foreign assets from which we borrow is very like a common pool resource, perhaps we need to control access more carefully to avoid traditional congestion problems. For each individual borrower or lender, access to international lending and borrowing offers individual benefits. Adverse impacts on credit ratings and policy discretion are congestion costs borne collectively. Administrative mechanisms for co-ordination or control of individual transactions, or an appropriate premium levied on such transactions, might better signal the social cost of individual optimizing decisions and bring these decisions more in line with collective welfare.

In addition to such emergency measures or the introduction of a more substantial wealth tax, we might consider a further step—to a continuing tax on international currency transactions. In the 1994 *Human Development Report*,[47] Nobel laureate James Tobin reminds us of his 1978 proposal for a uniform tax levied on all spot transactions in foreign exchange. He suggests that a 0.5% tax on foreign exchange transactions would focus attention on economic fundamentals rather than speculative opportunities and would slow speculative capital movements without deterring commodity trade or serious international capital commitments. Such a transactions tax, it is argued, would be designed to make international money markets compatible with modest national autonomy. (He does, however, note that such a tax would have to be worldwide to avoid evasion by executing transactions in havens where the tax deliberately did not exist. The proceeds of such an international tax would, he argued, appropriately be directed to international purposes.) While the immediate practical relevance of this suggestion in the Canadian setting may be limited, Canadian support of efforts to reach international agreement on such a tax is perhaps an appropriate part of a longer-term strategy and would have some significance in attempting to deal with concerns about a loss of national sovereignty in social policy fields.

Ide and Cordell[48] advocate a technology productivity tax to distribute the productivity gains inherent in the new technology, thereby maintaining an effective demand for goods and services. They argue that advances in productivity must be distributed more broadly if we are to avoid economic collapse. "The productivity of workers is now to be found in the productivity of technology. . . . Some of the gains in productivity must be taxed to create and maintain [public] infrastructure . . . and to provide a basic level of income." They make a case in particular for a "bit tax" levied on a new tax base, the bitstream—"that myriad of transactions, images, voice, text, data—all carried over global telecommunication, cable, and satellite networks."[49]

So as we look at the question of taxable capacity and the feasibility of financing a continuing social contract in Canada, certain avenues seem to call for sceptical further examination before we conclude that the social policy envelope must be gutted to solve the deficit problem:

1. Given that we are, in terms of ratios of total tax revenue to GDP, little higher than the G7 or OECD average, indeed just about the middle of either list, is it really true that we could find no support in Canada for increased taxes, particularly if earmarked for widely understood and endorsed purposes?

2. Given that we rely relatively little on charges or indirect taxes on corporations, is it really true that we could find no acceptance for increased charges for infrastructure or ecological services rendered in production, recognizing that such charges would improve resource allocation and promote sustainable enterprise while generating revenue to support investment in sustaining national wealth?

3. Finally, given the growing importance and awareness of critical social and natural capital assets as determinants of long-term competitiveness and comparative advantage, do we really need to be as worried as we are that capital and enterprise will readily find greener fields outside our borders?

The point, ultimately, is the need to find effective institutions to think further ahead about mutual interests—to recognize, beyond self-interest as revealed by short-term market calculations, some longer-term shared interests signalled by ethical guidelines that have evolved over a longer history. Of course, it is easy to point to experience that suggests that "short-term pain for long-term gain" is not a very persuasive slogan in economic—and, far less, political—affairs. But economists also provide compelling evidence that even on their own terms, conventional economic guidelines for the calculation of self-interest are not well founded.[50] Experience with processes of shared decision-making suggest some basis for optimism that longer-term social interests can sometimes be reflected in collective decisions that reconcile apparently conflicting short-term interests, even if these decisions demand that parties act as citizens in the public interest rather than economic agents pursuing individual interests.

Rethinking Fiscal Federalism: Roles of Governments

For purposes of this chapter, looking to medium- and longer-term issues, it has to be assumed that Quebec will remain part of a looser federation, which has succeeded in a substantial disentanglement of existing programs and responsibilities. It also has to be assumed that it will be possible for federal, provincial, territorial and First Nations governments to negotiate co-operative arrangements for the division both of tax powers and of jurisdiction or responsibility.

In broad-brush terms, without pretending to any exhaustive enumeration of program roles or calculation of financial balances, a general division of responsibilities consistent with the disentanglement sought emerges from the foregoing discussion. In this division, the federal government would exercise its taxing and spending powers directly to define the fundamental sharing and pooling of risks that flow from membership in the Canadian community. Through an integrated income tax and transfer system, the federal government would deliver a minimum participation income. Indeed, this program would become in large part the defining rationale for the national government in a situation where its role may otherwise be seen as substantially eroding.

The federal government role would also include continued responsibility for equalization programs, for ensuring effective functioning of the economic union and for the articulation of national standards as common goals for programs across the community.

Disentanglement of program responsibilities would be achieved through devolution to provincial, territorial and First Nations governments of responsibilities for additional support for individuals clearly not expected to work and for community-based social services. The last, in turn, would likely be devolved or contracted to organizations and groups in the voluntary sector or the informal economy.

In particular, provincial and local governments would hold

responsibility for community economic development, resource management and sustainability. Programs for conservation, habitat restoration, environmental monitoring and the like, financed by increased resource rents and ecological taxes, would provide a foundation of skills development, retraining and experience that would support the transition from school to work or from temporary unemployment to work.

The disparity between fiscal capacity and statutory social obligations has grown substantially over the past two decades, increasing the pressure on federal and provincial governments to undertake significant reforms for fiscal transfers and program designs. In 1986, Courchene cautioned that this reform must be embraced in a collaborative manner: "It is far preferable for Ottawa and the provinces to fall back on co-operative federalism and develop a coherent, co-ordinated policy to meet these challenges while time is still on their side than to be dragged into a series of stop-gap policies in times of fiscal or social policy crisis."[51] Eight years later, with crisis closer upon us, co-operation is still preferable.

An approach that seems persuasive has been outlined by Mintz and Wilson.[52] They suggest that the allocation of tax powers should reflect the division of expenditure responsibilities, and therefore that sales and excise taxes should be devolved to the provinces (ideally, perhaps, with a fully harmonized GST being collected at the provincial level), while wealth and capital taxes, tariffs and corporate income tax fields would be occupied by the federal government. Environmental taxes and the personal income tax would be co-responsibilities (with the latter collected by the federal government under appropriate agreements).

Canadian social policy has become increasingly important as a means of linking the country in some shared project. In attempting to deal with reform of the social security system in Canada, the federal government has a role to play in setting national standards for income security. The National Council of Welfare[53] has suggested five guiding principles that are relevant to all existing provincial and territorial welfare systems: adequacy, simplicity, accessibility, equity and due process. These principles provide common ground to satisfy the equity and efficiency requirements of policy reform by furnishing the economic union with uniform rules and benefits that establish fundamental citizenship entitlements and by ensuring that economic choices in areas such as trade, investment and mobility are not prejudiced by non-market factors.

Conclusion

This chapter has asked what sort of rethinking of economic management and social policy might emerge if we took seriously in aggregate what is increasingly widely recognized in bits and pieces— that our price mechanisms are seriously flawed in their representation of the values of ecological resources and services; that our accounting frameworks are dramatically incomplete in their failure to incorporate the values of natural resources and the significance of work in the home, the community and the voluntary sector; that our systems of property rights lack any satisfactory machinery for the conservation of natural capital and elements of the global commons; that our concepts of participation, contribution and wealth creation are distorted and dysfunctional; and that our distributional mechanisms fail to meet minimal standards of distributive justice.

Given these profound limitations of our present social and economic performance indicators, our generally accepted tests of economic value and fiscal viability are, for all but short-term bookkeeping, not simply meaningless: they are perverse. Tests of commercial viability are momentary and myopic, almost certainly misleading as measures of wealth creation or enduring economic value. The market is the most effective social innovation imaginable to serve the needs of a civilization wishing to decentralize almost all the tasks of economic management. The main claim here, however, is that the market is *not* the fundamental reality with which we must deal in rethinking social policy. The deficits of greatest concern are not the fiscal deficits as measured by accountants (without reference to public assets) or by economists (without reference to social or natural capital). They are the social deficit, capturing the shortfall in our investment in people and social structure, and the sustainability deficit, revealing how far short we fall from maintaining the capital that is the common heritage of humankind. The "wall" with which we must be concerned for purposes of public policy in the long run is not the wall of debt service constraints, but the wall of ecological carrying capacity. It may be that this latter wall is not ultimately a binding constraint or a reason for pessimism about maintenance of living standards; it may be that a viable path of sustainable development based on continuing technological innovation can be found. But it will not be found without massive revision of our market models. (And it is doubtful that it can be found without massive revision in lifestyle in the industrialized North. But that is another story.)

Three new features of the economic and social context have emerged within which the system of social support must now operate:

1. Economic and social restructuring have meant that labour markets, family structures and income generation mechanisms are not what they once were. Therefore, we have entered a world of unprecedented uncertainty, insecurity and vulnerability in employment and family support.

2. The present scale of human activity has brought us to the ecological limits or carrying capacity of the biosphere. Therefore, we have entered the "full world economy," where ecological resources and natural capital are scarce and crucial to production.

3. The information revolution that has moved us to the knowledge-based economy has also moved us to the borderless market and the information society, where transboundary influences give rise to the globalization of civil society (though, sadly, perhaps not the civilization of global society) and put immense premium on democratic and social participation through access to the machinery of the information society. In effect, the distributional concerns arising out of restricted or unequal access to information and communications capabilities have become increasingly central.

What becomes clear in this setting is that social policy is a concern for us all, needing security in an uncertain and volatile adaptive process, and not just a concern for the destitute, needing a hand out of poverty. Social policy must be directed toward assuring for all the opportunity for a recognized and respected role in society, for participation in the information society and for participation in the emerging civil society in which the wealth creation activities of the informal economy are recognized. At the same time, the distributional issues arising out of the concern for future generations (that is, the concern for sustainability) must also be addressed. What this analysis makes clear is that we must create the social institutions in which the machinery of the market can be properly directed, and that we must set these social institutions properly in the context of the natural systems that support them. Thus can economic, social and ecological sustainability be pursued in human decision-making. The concept of human security makes sense in no other context.

Resource Taxes and Green Dividends: A Combined Package

By James Robertson

The Context

PRESSURES ARE GROWING for a general restructuring of taxation and welfare benefits. At present they penalise employment and favour energy-intensive processes. They thus encourage inefficient use of resources—over-use of natural resources (including the environment's capacity to absorb pollution and waste), and under-use and under-development of human resources. By failing to discourage environmentally unsustainable activities, they fail to encourage innovation for sustainability and a larger share of the growing world market for environmental technologies and services. The benefits system discourages useful unpaid work like parenting. Means-tested benefits discourage saving, as well as earning. They create poverty and unemployment traps which lead to increasing social exclusion and rising costs for education, health, and law and order. Costs of the welfare state are already at crisis level in many countries.

For the future, international economic competition will continue to demand lower taxes on personal incomes and business profits in order to attract inward investment. In an ageing society, it will be more difficult to tax fewer people of working age on the fruits of their employment and enterprise in order to support a growing number of "economically inactive" people.

That, in brief, is the context for the proposal to combine:

- ecotax reform (i.e., a shift of taxation away from employment, incomes and savings, on to resource-depleting and environmentally damaging activities),
- the further replacement of existing taxes by another resource tax—a tax on land site-values, and
- the introduction of a Citizen's Income.

94

This combination would be phased in over a period of years. It would embody a new social compact between citizen and society for a new era of equitable and sustainable development, in which full employment of the conventional kind, a welfare state of the conventional kind, and economic growth of the conventional kind, were increasingly seen as questionable goals.

Ecotax Reform

Environmental taxation is now on the mainstream political agenda of the European Union and its member nations. To take one example, the July 1997 Statement of Intent by the present British Chancellor of the Exchequer, Gordon Brown, said: "The Government will explore the scope for using the tax system to deliver environmental objectives . . . Over time, the Government will aim to reform the tax system to increase incentives to reduce environmental damage. That will shift the burden of tax from "goods" to "bads"; encourage innovation in meeting higher environmental standards; and deliver a more dynamic economy and a cleaner environment, to the benefit of everyone."

Environmental taxes have tended to be seen as pollution taxes, based on the "polluter pays" principle. In economists' jargon, they aim to "internalise" costs previously "externalised" by polluters.

Understood more broadly, they are taxes on the use of resources—including the environment's capacity to absorb pollution and wastes. Energy taxes, water charges, and traffic congestion charges are other resource taxes. The principle is that people should pay for the benefits they get from using valuable resources created by nature or society and not by themselves. For example, in its 1995 Report the British Government Panel on Sustainable Development supported taxing people "on the value they subtract" rather than "the value they add."

Ecotax reform broadens the approach further. It is concerned not just with what environmental "bads" are to be taxed, but with how the revenue from the taxes should be used. The European Commission's White Paper on Growth, Competitiveness, Employment of December 1993 proposed to use ecotax revenues to reduce taxes on employment. This approach has now been developed in many official studies and reports, and has in some instances (as in the UK's landfill tax) been applied in practice.

Must Ecotaxation Be Regressive?

If existing taxes on incomes, profits and savings are simply replaced with environmental and resource taxes on consumers, they will hit poorer people relatively harder than richer. Regardless of the taxes they replace, ecotaxes are bound to have this regressive effect if they are applied "downstream" at the point of consumption. For example,

- value-added tax (VAT) on household energy hits poorer households harder than richer ones, because they do not have the money to pay the higher cost of the tax or to invest in greater energy efficiency; and
- similarly, fees and charges to reduce urban congestion will hurt small tradespeople who need to use their vehicles for their work, but will be painlessly absorbed by users of chauffeur-driven limousines.

If ecotaxes are to replace existing taxes significantly, this problem will have to be solved. How?

First, ecotaxes should, as far as possible, be applied "upstream." Of key importance will be a tax on carbon-energy (or on fossil fuels and nuclear energy), collected at source, cascading down through the economy, and raising the cost of the energy content of all goods and services. It will reduce pollution, because pollution arises predominantly from energy-intensive activities. It will be administratively simpler and easier to understand than a proliferation of separate ecotaxes on individual consumers and polluters. And, by raising costs for producers (as well as prices for consumers) of energy-intensive goods and services, it will be seen to impact richer people's incomes—salaries, dividends, capital appreciation, etc. It will thus be seen to be fairer and less discriminatory than taxes on consumers only. But, even so, ecotaxes will still be regressive, unless the regressive effect is offset in other ways.

So, second, ecotax reform should include a site-value tax on land. That is a resource tax that is progressive. It is not the poor who are enriched by the "enclosure" of the value of land.

And, third, the revenue from ecotaxes should be used progressively. To quote two examples, a 1994 German study concluded that, if part of the revenue from an energy tax were distributed to households as an ecobonus, the change would have positive economic and employment effects, and would reduce the net tax burden on low-income households; and a 1989 Swiss study concluded that if the revenue from levying two Swiss francs per litre of petrol were distributed to all adults as an ecobonus, people driving less than 7,000 kilometres a year would benefit, while people driving more would lose.

So, could ecobonuses add up to a Citizen's Income? And could a Citizen's Income be financed from from resource tax revenues? The answer is Yes. We come back to it later.

Site-Value Land Taxation

The proposal is to tax the annual rental site value of land. That does not include the value of developments carried out by the owner and his predecessors (which should not be taxed). It is the value of the land as provided by nature and as affected by the activities and regulations of society. Estimates for Britain in 1990 suggested the relative size of these values (£bn) for various land uses: housing 66.4; commerce 19.0; public services 10.2; industry 9.3; farm, woodland and forest 2.4. This tax has attracted favourable comment from economists since Adam Smith. Ricardo (1817) pointed out that a "tax on rent would affect rent only; it would fall wholly on landlords and could not be shifted to any class of consumers." In 1879, in *Progress and Poverty,* the American economist, Henry George, showed that to shift the burden of taxation from production and exchange to the value of land would stimulate employment and the production of wealth; the selling price of land would fall; land speculation would receive its death-blow; and land monopolisation would no longer pay. Leading economists since then have agreed that the tax on economic rent is the most neutral and most efficient of all taxes, inducing no distortions and generating no loss of welfare. Various political parties in Europe during the 20th century have included it in their policies, and it provides a component of local taxation in a number of countries today. But mainstream economic policy analysts in recent years have been strangely uninterested in it.

Just a case of normal professional groupthink? Or the consequence of an intellectual conspiracy inspired by American landowning interests early this century? Or a bit of both?

Some advocates of the site value tax have insisted that, as the "single tax" needed to finance all public spending, it should replace all others. Today, its more credible advocates present it as one important resource tax among others. Their arguments for a system of public finance based on socialising (i.e., taxing) the rent of land and other natural resources, and privatising (i.e., not taxing) people's wages and savings, appear wholly convincing.

Citizen's Income (or Basic Income)

The proposal is to distribute a Citizen's Income (CI)—often known as a basic income—as a tax-free income paid by the state to every man, woman and child as a right of citizenship. It will be age-related, with more for adults than children and more for elderly people than working-age adults.

CI for children will replace today's child benefit, and CI for the elderly will replace today's state pensions. There will be supplements for disability, housing benefits, and other exceptional circumstances. Otherwise CI will replace all existing benefits and tax allowances. The amount of a person's CI will be unaffected by their income or wealth, their work status, gender or marital status.

In Britain, advocates of a basic income have included Tom Paine in the 1790s, John Stuart Mill in the 19th century, Major C.H. Douglas in the 1920s, and distinguished economists like Samuel Brittan and James Meade more recently. Support for it continues to grow in many European countries. A recent study, quoting the principle that "Nature and its resources are for the benefit of all," showed that a full basic income could be introduced in Ireland over a period of three budgets, resulting in

- nobody receiving less than the poverty line of income,
- all unemployment and poverty traps being eliminated, and
- it always being worthwhile for an unemployed person to take up a job.

Until recently the assumption was that a basic income would be financed out of income tax. But a shift of opinion within the European basic income movement towards financing it from "sources reflecting a 'common endowment'" is now apparent.

Targeting or Universality?

At first sight, it seems sensible to target benefits to those who need them, rather than distribute them to everyone. But targeting involves means testing to establish need and eligibility. And means testing has serious disadvantages. For example,

- it is demeaning and socially divisive;
- to avoid it, many people fail to take up benefits to which they are entitled;
- it tightens the unemployment and poverty traps, by reducing incentives to earn and save; and
- people who have earned and saved enough to disqualify them from benefits, resent "scroungers" who have not.

The universality of a Citizen's Income avoids these social and economic disadvantages. The objections to it have been that:

- the total direct cost of CI to government will be higher than that of selective benefits based on means-tested need; and
- people in general should not receive unearned "hand-outs from the state"—whereas the element in the unearned incomes of rich and

middle-income people, that is based directly or indirectly on "enclosure" of the value of common resources, is accepted as perfectly in order.

These objections can be met by combining a CI with a restructured tax system, whereby:

- taxes on the use or monopolisation of common resources will recover the value of the CI (or more) from rich people; and
- CI will be seen as every citizen's share of the value of common resources.

The result will be doubly progressive. The CI will be progressive because the same amount of money is worth relatively more to poor people than rich. The taxes will be progressive because they will impact richer people both in terms of their spending and in terms of their incomes and wealth. Their higher spending as consumers will mean they will pay more than poorer people, for example for the energy that has been used in producing the goods and services they buy. The larger proportion of their incomes and wealth (salaries, dividends, capital growth, etc.) derived directly or indirectly from land ownership and the use of other common resources like energy, will mean they pay proportionately more tax (indirectly) on their incomes.

Towards a New Social Compact

The question, then, is whether the transition to an economically sound, socially just and environmentally sustainable future should involve a package of reforms based on:

- the introduction of higher taxes and charges on the use of common resources and values, particularly including energy and the site value of land;
- the reduction, and perhaps the eventual abolition, of taxes and charges on employment, incomes, profits, value added, and capital; and
- the introduction of a Citizen's Income, to which ecobonuses will contribute, paid to all citizens as of right in place of all tax reliefs and many existing welfare benefits.

The ecotax reform movement has been gathering strength in mainstream policy-making and academic research but still faces serious problems. The movements for site-value taxation and Citizen's Income are growing stronger. Over the next few years the potential synergies between the three will become clearer. Beyond the practical arguments for treating them as a package, an integrating vision may emerge.

It would be a vision of a people-centred society—less employer-centred and state-centred than today's. Its citizens, more equal with one another in esteem, capability and material conditions of life than now, would all be entitled to share in the value of the common resources created by nature and society as a whole. It would be a vision of a society:

- which does not tax people for what they earn by their useful work and enterprise, by the value they add, and by what they contribute to the common good;
- in which the amounts that people and organisations pay to the public revenue reflect the value they subtract by their use or monopolisation of common resources; and
- in which all citizens are equally entitled to share in the annual revenue so raised, partly by way of public services and partly as a Citizen's Income.

While citizens of such a society would more easily get paid work, they would no longer be so dependent as now on employers to provide them with incomes and to organise their work. The modern-age class division between employers and employees would fade—as the old master/slave and lord/serf relationships of ancient and medieval societies have faded. It would be normal for people to work for themselves and one another. The aim in many fields of policy would be to enable people to manage their own working lives.

The social compact of the employment age may be breaking down. The time may be passing when the great majority of citizens, excluded from access to land and other means of production and from their share of common resources and values, could nevertheless depend on employers to provide them with incomes in exchange for work, and on the state for special benefits to see them through exceptional periods of unemployment. For the future, all citizens may be expected to take greater responsibility for themselves and their contribution to society, in exchange for recognition of their right to share in the value of the "commons." Combining resource taxes with green dividends would help to underpin a new social compact on those lines.

Additional readings

O'Riordan, T. (ed.). *Ecotaxation.* London: Earthscan, 1997.

Robertson, James. *Beyond the Dependency Culture.* London: Adamantine Press, 1998.

von Weizsacker, Ernst Ulrich. *Earth Politics.* London: Zed Books, 1994.

Excerpted from

SEEKING EQUALITY OF SECURITY IN THE ERA OF GLOBALISATION

By Guy Standing

ALL OVER THE WORLD governments have been cutting social benefits and making them more selective, in the name of cutting public expenditure and "targeting," which means more means-testing, tighter conditions and so on. Social protection is being partially privatised, and economic and social *insecurity* is becoming pervasive.

It is important to recognise that economic dynamism may be improved. If so, let us celebrate that, as long as it is ecologically and socially beneficial. What one should be worried about are the social, ecological and societal costs of the era of market regulation, including the human development costs of growing inequalities and insecurities. Against that, one must recall optimistically that every era of insecurity has led to an era of redistributive struggle and some success. We need a *new vision* of redistributive justice to guide that phase.

What would be the appropriate redistributive strategy? Where do we find a coherent vision of the future, and what organisations could provide the necessary leadership and pressure? We must start by reflecting on how the intellectual world has changed as globalisation has proceeded in the 1990s. We feel uncomfortable with words and ideas that for centuries have guided social progress—words like equality. The anger is missing. Perhaps now, more than at any time, the privileged, which includes most intellectuals, feel *detached*—comfortable—detached from the fears, insecurities, aspirations and values of the poor and dispossessed. The tenuous connection of social solidarity has been always fundamentally an *emotional* tie that comes from a sense of common history, from the past and into the future. Now we see a more sharply *fragmented* society, a global society, in which *we* are not *them*. Economic change, technology, labour market flexibility, politics have all helped in this fragmentation. But there it is.

If social progress is to resume—and it will—social and economic distance between social groups and vested interests, between workers and others, must shrink. A new coalition must evolve, a coalition of people who believe strongly that redistributive justice is required *and* feasible, and in some cases worth sacrificing personal interest to obtain. Fear will not change sides again until that happens.

A new strategy to achieve distributive justice must seek *equality of security* and *good opportunity* in society. We must begin by rejecting claims that insecurity and inequality are functional or inevitable. We must accept that labour is a means to an end, not an end to be idealised. We must stand on the Rawlsian Difference Principle, that reforms are justifiable only if they improve the position of the worst-off groups in society. For their part, workers and unions must escape from the tendency to believe that differences in income between those on the margins of the labour market and those in employment should be large. The incentive to work should not be fear, but hope.

There must be recognition that for a growing proportion of the population in most middle-income and industrialised societies, income security will not be possible through labour force participation alone. Finally, a health warning should be attached to any proposal to strengthen "active" labour market or social policy. The paternalistic desire to regulate the behaviour of the poor and unemployed in ways policymakers and bureaucrats think are appropriate should be treated with suspicion. There should be better training and employment *services* available, as opportunities. But nobody should be coerced or driven by fear and insecurity to opt for those policies.

The redistributive strategy should be based on a reconsideration of security. The strategy should aim to equalise basic security, while not undermining the incentive to work, save and invest. It must promote individual *liberty*, while promoting the sense of *community* and social solidarity. The freedom must be based on individual self-control, which can only be achieved with basic personal security. That is why *income security* is fundamental to any decent vision of the future.

The difficulty is that the instruments for obtaining income security in the twentieth century will be inappropriate for the twenty-first. It will be necessary to move away from the patchwork of inefficient, inequitable and regulatory social protection mechanisms that have come to characterise the late twentieth century. We must escape from the pernicious euphemisms that have been part of the neo-liberal agenda, such as "social safety net" and "targeting."

In the longer term, income security will only be achieved by gradually delinking the provision of basic income security from labour conditionality. In other words, providing a modest income to people should not be made conditional on taking jobs. A modest *unconditional* citizenship income should be guaranteed as a right, a dignity income, paid individually for all men and women, without conditions, without obligations, regardless of labour status, marital status or age (with a lower amount for children and supplements for those with disability or special needs). This will not come at once, and must be seen as a trend to pursue. Beyond that, as far as possible, improving individual lifestyle and pursuing work as occupation should be the responsibility of people themselves, assisted by their representative organisations and communities.

Moving in the direction of a basic citizenship income grant would be the first part of a redistributive strategy, which could be justified on moral, philosophical, economic and political grounds. However, let me merely devote a few moments to the main criticisms and main advantages of moving in that direction.

The first criticism is *cost*. Surely, critics say, it would be far too expensive to give everyone a basic survival income. There are various responses to this. One could refer to priorities, pointing to the obvious fact that governments spend high proportions of national incomes. Beyond that, note that a citizenship income would replace many existing or envisaged state transfers, and would not simply be an additional expenditure. It would also reduce administrative costs, which are high in any social protection system where regulating and selectivity are important activities. It would also reduce poverty traps and unemployment traps—whereby many of the poor and near-poor are discouraged from working legally or saving because they would lose existing means-tested benefits—and would thus enable and encourage more people at the lower end of the earnings spectrum to work for income, so raising taxable incomes and spending.

A citizenship income could be funded in part through social endowment funds, in part from the proceeds of privatisation schemes, in part from taxing the surplus received from those making super-profits from monopoly rents from technological progress. There are many ways, including the proposed Tobin tax and ecological taxes, by which a modest move to a citizenship income could be financed. Ultimately, one must ask three questions: "Can society afford to provide its citizens with an income on which to survive? Do we want to afford it? How could we do it?" If we answer yes to the first two questions, then it should not be too difficult to find a feasible answer to the third.

A second criticism is that it would result in workers being paid lower wages. This is mistaken, simply because it is fear and insecurity that leads to workers accepting terribly low wages. Having the assurance of basic income security would actually enable workers to say no with greater ease when confronted with sub-subsistence wages.

A third criticism is that an unconditional citizenship income would undermine the incentive to labour. This is an insult to human motivation. People everywhere want to better themselves. The vast majority would not be satisfied with a very basic income. And by removing the poverty traps and unemployment traps, the incentive to take a wage job would actually be increased. It would also put pressure on employers to improve the type of job on offer and raise wages at the bottom so as to make employment more attractive. The criticism also invites a sarcastic retort: The critics never seem to argue that money should be taken from the leisurely rich to strengthen their incentive to labour. Finally, *if* a few people did prefer to opt for a low-income, high-"leisure" lifestyle, the social cost would be negligible since the productivity of this type of person is likely to be very low, and in conditions of labour surplus others could take the available jobs.

The main advantage of moving in the direction of a citizenship income is that it is the only way of providing income security for the poor and near-poor that is compatible with freedom and human dignity. It would lessen or remove the *stigma* of social transfers. It would remove the policing of the poor by means tests, behaviour tests and so on. It would also make the system of social protection more transparent. It would be administratively simple, with no large transaction costs and no moral hazards, in contrast to the present situation where potential recipients of state transfers around the world often have a vested interest in lying about their circumstances and behaviour. It would also be consistent with the promotion of more flexible life styles, implicitly recognising the value of other forms of *work* as well as income-earning labour. Finally, as a distributional instrument, it would reflect a corrective mechanism for the growing inequalities due to the nature of rapid technological progress and increased income accruing to capital. And it would compensate for the privatisation of social policy, which *may* have efficiency arguments in its favour but which is surely inegalitarian in its outcomes.

Now an important caveat: A citizenship income must not be presented or understood as a panacea. It is only part of a redistributive strategy that would be consistent with globalisation and more flexible product and labour markets. Without other components, it would be rather ineffectual.

The second part is *economic democracy*. The premises are that income accruing to capital and to those making technological advance has been rising, while the income going to labour has been lagging.[1] Taxes on capital are becoming more ineffectual and are being cut as a result of globalisation and other forces.[2] And we are seeing a global trend towards "flexible" pay systems based on individualised profit sharing, profit-related pay, performance-related pay and so on, which are widening earnings differentials. Ordinary workers and their families and communities are being left behind, as well as the unemployed, the flexiworkers and the lumpenised elements in society.

The most feasible option for reversing this divisive trend is to incorporate workers, unions and their communities into the dynamic economic mainstream as *stakeholders*, so as to enable them to share the economic surplus with those currently gaining from capital. Research around the world has shown that profit sharing can have beneficial effects for investment and income distribution. It can encourage longer-term investment, rather than the rapid dispersion of profits to external principals, shareholders who are not directly involved in the production process. It can encourage more training investment by the firm. Many benefits could be gained, *if the design of the surplus sharing is appropriate.*

First and foremost, the surplus sharing system must be wider than the company or plant level. Surplus must be shared with the flexiworkers who are intermittently in employment and it must be shared with the community around the firm. Among the benefits of this would be that income inequalities between those inside and outside employment would be reduced, and social pressures would be placed on those not in employment to play the role of socially responsible citizens. Firms would benefit from an enlarged pool of skilled workers, given the increased training in the firm and the social pressure to make the training generalised for the benefit of the community.

A *communal profit sharing* system should provide adequate incentives to invest and reinvest and all those bargaining over the share system would have a direct interest in strengthening the companies. Indeed, this should be part of the character of good firms. Elsewhere the proposal is made that what might be called *Human Development Enterprises* should be encouraged through incentives, public Awards, priority in the award of public contracts, and so on.[3] If these two policies were developed together workers would benefit through being able to exercise more control in and around the workplace, they would be more inclined to favour technological advance, they would be better placed to check opportunistic practices by managements or outsiders and they would want dynamically efficient companies.

Finally, what about unions themselves? No redistributive agenda will succeed or be safe unless there is strong *Voice Regulation*, strong organisations representing the vulnerable in society. The unions themselves must change. Neither craft unions, nor industrial unions nor company (or enterprise) unions will be able to represent the flexible labour forces of the future. The future should have *community unions*, which may need to shed their name in favour of something that reflects their new functions and objectives. They should bargain on behalf of today's workers as workers, on behalf of tomorrow's potential workers from the community, and on behalf of both as broader stakeholders in the production process. They will have to represent those on the margins as well as those in secure jobs. Otherwise they will end up representing neither. Beyond community unions, there will need to be national federations of such unions and international federations to work out common strategies.

To conclude: Every era of capitalist triumphalism creates the basis for renewed social struggle to ameliorate inequalities, a struggle to limit the new mechanisms of inequality. Every technological revolution has been accompanied by ruling elites calling for more flexibility (or whatever the word at the time) from workers and for more "discipline" over them. In such times, momentarily, the forward march of social progress seems to be halted, even reversed. Then, once a vision of an alternative, viable system of distributive justice has crystallised, the state has moved in that direction, to re-embed the economy in society. Then—perhaps in directions that were not previously foreseen—the forward march resumes.

NOTES

1 The Need for Basic Economic Security

1 See, for example, Duffy, Glenday and Pupo 1997; Greider 1997; Wolman and Colamosca 1997; Reid 1996; Korten 1995; Rifkin 1995; Simai 1995; Aronowitz and Difazio 1994; Barnet and Cavanagh 1994; Freeman and Soete 1994; Lerner 1994; Lipietz 1992; Reich 1992.

2 What Is Basic Income?

1 Members of BIEN, an organization that has been studying the concept of BI for fifteen years, have provided and organized much of the research that we will draw upon in examining the BI concept. Their biennial meetings and quarterly newsletter have created a strong network of BI scholars and advocates whose work promotes constructive debate on the why and how of different approaches to BI. More information about BIEN and details on joining can be found at:
http://www.espo.ucl.ac.be/ETES/BIEN/bien.html

2 "Coinciding with the federal-provincial review of social security in the mid-seventies, Canada and Manitoba jointly financed an evaluation of the guaranteed income concept. The experiment, known as MINCOME MANITOBA, was designed to investigate work incentives as well as administrative issues. . . . Over 1300 families in the City of Winnipeg, the town of Dauphin and a number of rural communities in Manitoba participated in the project and were guaranteed an annual income for three years. Because no one could say in advance what the effects of different support levels and tax back rates on the desire to work, a number of combinations were tried. Three guarantee levels were tested: $3800, $4800 and $5800 (1975 prices) for a family of four. Three tax back rates were also specified: 35%, 50% and 75%. The experiments terminated in 1979 after amassing quantities of data, but before completion of the intended program of research." D. Hum, "UISP and the Macdonald Commission: Reform and Restraint," *Canadian Public Policy*, 12 (1986, supplement): 99. Also see: A. Basilevsky and D. Hum, *Experimental Social Programs and Analytic Methods: An Evaluation of the U.S. Income Maintenance Projects* (New York: Academic Press, 1984).

3 D. Hum and W. Simpson, *Income Maintenance Work Effort, and the Canadian Mincome Experiment* (Ottawa: Minister of Supply and Services Canada, 1991), xvi. The Canadian results of Hum and Simpson, published by the Economic Council of Canada, are from data from the Manitoba Basic Annual Income Experiment (Mincome) of which Hum was Research Director from 1975-1979. Hum and Simpson also analyzed empirically based U.S. studies (see pages 35-39).

4 G. Berlin, W. Bancroft, D. Card, W. Lin and P. K. Robins, *Do Work Incentives Have Unintended Consequences? Measuring "Entry Effects" in the Self-Sufficiency Project* (Ottawa and Vancouver: Social Research and Demonstration Corporation, March 1998), viii.

5 Ibid., 38.

3   Basic Income in the Canadian Policy Context

1 D. Smiley, ed., *The Rowell-Sirois Report*, 1963, pp. 185-87. "This was the 1937 Report of the Royal Commission on Dominion-Provincial Relations, the first effort to create a structure of 'equalization' payments between federal and provincial governments and have and have-not provinces." (Yalnizyan, 1994, 68 n.5).

2 D. Bellamy, "Social Welfare in Canada," *Encyclopedia of Social Work* (New York: National Association of Social Workers, 1965). J. W. Willard, "Canadian Welfare Programmes," *Encyclopedia of Social Work* (New York: National Association of Social Workers, 1965). A. Armitage, *Social Welfare in Canada: Ideals and Realities* (Toronto: McClelland and Stewart, 1988). D. Guest, *The Emergence of Social Security in Canada*. (Vancouver: University of British Columbia Press, 1997).

3 A. Yalnizyan, T. R. Ide and A. J. Cordell, *Shifting Time: Social Policy and the Future of Work* (Toronto: Between the Lines, 1994), 35. Yalnizyan references: D. Hum, *Federalism and the Poor: A Review of the Canada Assistance Plan*. (Toronto: Ontario Economic Council, 1983), 19.

4 See: D. Hum, "UISP and the Macdonald Commission: Reform and Restraint," *Canadian Public Policy*, 12 (1986 supplement): 92-100. B. Kitchen with C. Frieler and J. Patterson, *A Guaranteed Income: A New Look at an Old Idea* (Toronto: Social Planning Council of Metropolitan Toronto, 1986).

5 In addition to being politically unacceptable because it did not squarely address justice issues, the UISP would probably have not been workable because of its technical complexity and incompleteness. Essentially a negative income tax device, it would have required a combination of federal and provincial programs, provided very low benefits, necessitating a low 20 percent tax back rate on earned income, but would have significantly increased marginal tax rates. See: B. Kitchen and others, *A Guaranteed Income: A New Look at an Old Idea* (Toronto: Social Planning Council of Metropolitan Toronto, 1986), 33; and J. R. Kesselman, "The Royal Commission's Proposals for Income Security Reform," *Canadian Public Policy* 12 (1986 supplement): 101-12.

5   A Canadian Basic Income Model

1 Some early examples of BI-type proposals for Canada can be found in *Guaranteed Annual Income: An Integrated Approach* (Ottawa: Canadian Council on Social Development, The Runge Press, 1973.)

2 For an example of what a complete proposal would look like, the reader can refer to the work of the Conference of the Religious of Ireland and their many publications on the proposal they have developed. See B. Reynolds and S. Healy, *Towards an Adequate Income for All*, 1994; *An Adequate Income Guarantee*, 1995; and *Progress, Values and Public Policy*, 1996; and C. Clark and J. Healy, *Pathways to a Basic Income*, 1997. Available from Justice Commission, CORI, Milltown Park, Dublin 6, Ireland.

Additional Readings

David Korten: Securing the Right to Live

1 John Locke, *The Second Treatise of Government*, chapter 5, paragraph 34, in David Wooten, *Political Writings of John Locke* (New York: Penguin, 1993), p. 277.

2 Locke, chapter 5, paragraph 25, p. 273.

3 Locke, chapter 5, paragraph 27, 25, p. 273-74.

4 Locke, chapter 5, paragraph 32, p. 276.

5 Locke, chapter 5, paragraph 25, p. 273.

6 Richard Ashcraft, "Locke's Political Philosophy," in Vere Chappell (ed.), *The Cambridge Companion to Locke* (Cambridge: Cambridge University Press, 1994), pp. 248-49.

Rod Dobell: The Dance of the Deficit and the Real World of Wealth

1 The expression "social capital" is used here in the formal sense suggested by Elinor Ostrom: Institutions or "rules in use" represent social capital, the creation of which demands expenditure of effort and resources and the presence of which assures a greater stream of returns to given stocks of physical, human and natural capital. See E. Ostrom, *Crafting Institutions for Self-Governing Irrigation Systems* (San Francisco: Institute for Contemporary Studies, 1992).

2 D. Quinn, *Ishmael* (Toronto: Bantam, 1992); E.O. Wilson, *The Diversity of Life* (Cambridge: Harvard University Press, 1992).

3 See M.C. Wolfson, "A Guaranteed Income," *Policy Options,* (January 1986): 35-45; and A.B. Atkinson, "Beveridge, the National Minimum, and Its Future in a European Context," Discussion Paper WSP/85, Welfare State Programme, STICERD (London: London School of Economics, 1993).

4 R.G. Lipsey, "Globalization, Technological Change and Economic Growth," *The Journal of Canadian Business Economics*, 2, 1 (Fall 1993): 3-17.

5 L. Osberg et al. *The Information Economy: The Implications of Unbalanced Growth* (Halifax: Institute for Research on Public Policy, 1989).

6 R. Morissette et al. "What is Happening to Earnings Inequality in Canada?," Research Paper 60 (Ottawa: Statistics Canada, Analytical Studies Branch, 1993).

7 C.M. Beach and G.A. Slotsve, "Polarization of Earnings in the Canadian Labour Market," in *Stabilization, Growth and Distribution: Linkages in the Knowledge Era*, edited by T.J. Courchene, The Bell Canada Papers on Economic and Public Policy (Kingston, ON: Queen's University, John Deutsch Institute for the Study of Economic Policy, 1994); M.C. Wolfson, "Divergent Inequalities—Theory, Empirical Results and Prescriptions," paper presented at the American Economics Association Meetings, Boston, 5 January 1994 (Ottawa: Statistics Canada, 1993).

8 J.M. Keynes, *A Treatise on Money* (1930), quoted by A.J. Cordell in *The Uneasy Eighties: The Transition to an Information Society*, Science Council of Canada, Background Study 53 (Ottawa: Ministry of Supply and Services, 1985).

9 British White Paper (1945), United States Employment Act (1946) and Canada's White Paper (1946).

10 Organization for Economic Cooperation and Development, *The OECD Jobs Study: Facts, Analysis, Strategies* (Paris: OECD, 1994).

11 OECD, *Jobs Study.*

12 Informal work encompasses the non-market economic activities of households and communities. It includes the legal production of food, clothing, shelter and heat for personal, familial and community use, child rearing, housework, home maintenance and renovations that are not contracted out, volunteer activity, mutual aid, barter, skills exchange and co-operative or collective enterprises. Certain characteristics of production and exchange in informal work are highly suited to the current economic environment; e.g., less money involved in transactions, decentralization, locally controlled production, more emphasis on co-operation, egalitarian information flows and strategic alliances, increased participation by women and youth, less emphasis on the profit motive and capital accumulation, and greater sensitivity to the effects of economic activity on the environment, on personal well-being and on relationships with others at work, home and in the community.

13 Lerner surveys these issues and possible policy responses in some detail. See S. Lerner, "The Future of Work in North America," *Futures*, 26, 2 (1994): 185-196.

14 A. Rotstein, *Rebuilding from Within* (Toronto: Lorimer, 1984).

15 A. Nakamura and P. Lawrence, "Education, Training and Prosperity," in *Stabilization, Growth and Distribution: Linkages in the Knowledge Era*, edited by T.J. Courchene, The Bell Canada Papers on Economic and Public Policy (Kingston, ON: Queen's University, John Deutsch Institute for the Study of Economic Policy, 1994).

16 International Union for the Conservation of Nature et al. *World Conservation Strategy: Living Resource Conservation for Sustainable Development* (Gland, Switzerland: IUCN, 1980).

17 D.W. Pearce et al. *Blueprint for a Green Economy* (London: Earthscan, 1989); Wolfson, "Divergent Inequalities"; M.C. Wolfson, "Implications of Evolutionary Economics for Measurement in the SNA: Towards a System of Social and Economic Statistics," prepared for the Conference of the International Association for Research in Income and Wealth, 21-27 August 1994 (Ottawa: Statistics Canada, 1994).

18 P. Hawken, *The Ecology of Commerce: A Declaration of Sustainability* (New York: HarperCollins, 1993).

19 B.R. Kennedy, "Real Reform in Income Security," *Policy Options* (November 1989): 9-12.

20 British Columbia Commission on Resources and Environment, *A Sustainability Act for British Columbia* (Victoria: Queen's Printer for British Columbia, 1994).

21 D. Ronfeldt and C. Thorup, "NGOs, Civil Society Networks, and the Future of North America," in *Transborder Citizens: Networks and New Institutions in North America*, edited by R. Dobell and M. Neufeld (Lantzville, BC: Oolichan Books, 1994).

22 M. Dorais, "Environmental Assessment: Consequences of the Emergence of Procedural Democracy," *Optimum*, 25, 3 (1995): 36-39.

23 Ostrom, *Crafting Institutions*.

24 Putnam et al. make a similar point on the basis of work on government, civil society and economic development in Italy; see R.D. Putnam et al., *Making Democracy Work: Civic Traditions in Modern Italy* (Princeton, NJ: Princeton University Press, 1993). In the world of evolutionary economics, with the heavy emphasis on institutional aspects of the innovation process (e.g., as suggested by Miller), the significance of social capital in determining the effectiveness of investment in innovation and learning seems evident; see R. Miller, "The New Worlds of Innovation: Diversity and Coherence," in *Stabilization, Growth and Distribution: Linkages in the Knowledge Era*, edited by T.J. Courchene (Kingston, ON: Queen's University, John Deutsch Institute for the Study of Economic Policy, 1994), 173-233.

25 J. Rhys-Williams, *Something to Look Forward To* (London: Macdonald, 1943), quoted by Atkinson in "Beveridge." Amended from the original to gender-neutral language.

26 M. Strong, "Building Bridges: Environment and the New North American Partnership," in *Environmental Cooperation in North America: National Policies, Transnational Scrutiny & International Institutions*, edited by A.R. Dobell (Lantzville, BC: Oolichan Books, 1994).

27 Wolfson, "A Guaranteed Income."

28 H. Parker, *Instead of the Dole: An Enquiry into the Integration of the Tax and Benefit Systems* (London: Routledge, 1989).

29 Atkinson, "Beveridge."

30 Wolfson, "A Guaranteed Income."

31 J.A. Brander, *Government Policy Toward Business* (Toronto and Vancouver: Butterworths, 1992).

32 Kennedy, "Real Reform."

33 United Nations Development Programme, *Human Development Report* (New York: Oxford University Press, 1994), 39.

34 Ignatieff reminds us that "in the welfare state, old divisions of class have been re-expressed as divisions between those dependent on the state, and those free to satisfy their needs in the market place." Such divisions may yet block any significant social policy reform in Canada, even in the longer term. See M. Ignatieff, *The Needs of Strangers* (London: Hogarth Press, 1984), 137.

35 See H. Daly, "The Perils of Free Trade," *Scientific American* (November 1993): 50-57, and International Institute for Sustainable Development, *Trade and Sustainable Development*, Appendix A (Winnipeg: IISD, 1992), 125-127, for an outline of the argument that, in a world of mobile factors of production, analyses based on comparative advantage no longer serve.

36 C. Clark, *Taxmanship: Principles and Proposals for the Reform of Taxation*, Hobart Paper 26 (London: Institute of Economic Affairs, 1964), 21.

37 D.B. Perry, "International Tax Comparisons, 1992," *Canadian Tax Journal*, 41 (1993): 1211-1221.

38 Organization for Economic Cooperation and Development, *Revenue Statistics of Member Countries* (Paris: OECD, 1993).

39 J.C. Strick, "Critical Limits to Taxation," *Canadian Tax Journal*, 40, 6 (1992): 1315-1331.

40 L. Trocki, "Science, Technology, Environment and Competitiveness in a North American Context," in *Harmonizing Economic Competitiveness with Environmental Quality: A North American Challenge* (Santa Fe: North American Institute, 1991).

41 See for example J.L. Knetsch, *Environmental Valuation: Some Practical Problems of Wrong Questions and Misleading Answers*, Occasional Publication 5 (Canberra: Resource Assessment Commission, 1993), and A.M. Rivlin, *Reviving the American Dream: The Economy, the State and the Federal Government* (Washington, DC: The Brookings Institution, 1992). An interesting example of the kind of public policy to which such reasoning can lead is offered by British Columbia's Forest Transition Strategy, the essence of which is to earmark revenues from increased stumpage fees and royalties for the use of publicly owned forest resources, and to direct those earmarked revenues to financing the adjustment process in the forest industry. The flaw in the economic reasoning here, of course, is that the owners of the resource are not only those in the forest industry but all the residents of the province, and the use of the revenues should underwrite the process of economic adjustment throughout the province.

42 D. Miller, "Decision Time on Climate Change," *National Round Table Review* (Winter 1995): 19.

43 R. Costanza, "Three General Policies to Achieve Sustainability," in *Investing in Natural Capital: The Ecological Economics Approach to Sustainability,* edited by A.M. Jansson et al. (Washington, DC: Island Press, 1994), 392-407; E.U. von Weizsacker and J. Jesinghaus, *Ecological Tax Reform: A Policy Proposal for Sustainable Development* (London: Zed Books, 1992).

44 B. Kennedy, "Real Reform in Income Security," *Policy Options* (November 1989): 9-12.

45 Hawken, *The Ecology of Commerce.*

46 L. Vallee, "Virtual Rescheduling: Solving the Debt/Deficit Problem," *Policy Options,* 16, 1 (January-February 1995): 36-39.

47 United Nations Development Programme, *Human Development Report* (New York: Oxford University Press, 1994), 70.

48 T.R. Ide and A.J. Cordell, "The New Tools: Implications for the Future of Work," in *Shifting Time: Social Policy and the Future of Work,* edited by Armine Yalnizyan (Toronto: Between the Lines, 1994).

49 A.J. Cordell and T.R. Ide, "The New Wealth of Nations: Distributing Prosperity," paper prepared for the Club of Rome annual meeting, Buenos Aires, November 30 - December 2, 1994, 33. Also, Costanza et al. emphasize the crucial importance of ecological tax reform; R. Costanza et al., "The Tax Shift: Non-Partisan Tax Reform," Ecol-Econ Discussion List [ecol-econ@csf.colorado.edu] (Colorado: Communications for a Sustainable Future, 13 March 1995).

50 D. Card and A. Krueger, *Myth and Measurement: The New Economics of the Minimum Wage* (Princeton: Princeton University Press, 1995); J.L. Knetsch, "Assumptions, Behavioural Findings, and Policy Analysis," *Journal of Policy Analysis and Management,* 14, 1 (1995): 68-78.

51 T.J. Courchene, *Economic Management and the Division of Powers,* published in co-operation with the Royal Commission on the Economic Union and Development Prospects for Canada (Toronto: University of Toronto Press, 1986), 123.

52 J.M. Mintz and T.A. Wilson, "The Allocation of Tax Authority in the Canadian Federation," paper prepared for the conference *Economic Dimensions of Constitutional Change* (Kingston: Queen's University, John Deutsch Institute for the Study of Economic Policy, 1991).

53 National Council of Welfare, *Welfare Reform: A Report* (Ottawa: National Council of Welfare, 1992).

Guy Standing: Seeking Equality of Security in the Era of Globalisation

1 Let me make an aside here. In the winner-takes-all type of labour market that is emerging, certain situations are becoming bizarre. It is recognised that Bill Gates made a pebble of a contribution to a Gibralter of technological advance in software; it was a useful pebble, but those who added the earlier bits received very little. In 1996, Gates' wealth was about $20 billion, making him the richest man in the world. By 1997, it was over $40 billion—or the equivalent of the national income of a country like Colombia. There is nothing to stop his wealth growing. Being sure that his wealth will combine with science to increase his longevity, by the middle of next century his wealth will be greater than the GNP of Brazil. Remember you heard that first here. [Gates' wealth passed the US$60 billion mark in 1999.]

2 Ironically, in many countries, while the share of national income going to profits has

risen, the share of tax revenue coming from capital has declined, and while the share of national income to labour has declined, the share of tax revenue coming from labour has gone up.

3 G.Standing, "The Human Development Enterprise: Seeking Flexibility and Security" (Geneva: ILO, 1996).

REFERENCES

Alperovitz, G. "Distributing Our Technological Inheritance." *Technology Review* (October 1994): 32-36.

Armitage, A. *Social Welfare in Canada: Ideals and Realities and Future Paths.* Toronto: McClelland and Stewart, 1975, 1988.

Aronowitz, S., and W. DiFazio. *The Jobless Future.* Minneapolis: University of Minnesota Press, 1994.

Barnet, R. J., and J. Cavanagh. *Global Dreams.* New York: Simon & Schuster, 1994.

Basic Income 28. Newsletter of the Basic Income European Network (Christmas 1997).

Basilevsky, A., and D. Hum. *Experimental Social Programs and Analytic Methods: An Evaluation of the U.S. Income Maintenance Projects.* New York: Academic Press, 1994.

Battle, K. "Back to the Future: Reforming Social Policy in Canada." Revision of paper presented at The Public Good: Lessons for the 3rd Millennium: A Conference in Honour of Allan J. MacEachen (July 6, 1996).

Beck, Ulrich. "Goodbye to All That Wage Slavery." *New Statesman,* May 3, 1999, Vol. 129, Issue 4426.

Bellamy, "Social Welfare in Canada." In *Encyclopedia of Social Work.* New York: National Association of Social Workers, 1965.

Berlin, G., W. Bancroft, D. Card, W. Lin and P. K. Robins. *Do Work Incentives Have Unintended Consequences? Measuring "Entry Effects" in the Self-Sufficiency Project.* Ottawa and Vancouver: Social Research and Demonstration Corporation, March 1998.

Betcherman, G., and G. Lowe. *The Future of Work in Canada—A Synthesis Report.* Ottawa: Canadian Policy Research Networks Inc., 1997.

Beveridge, W. *Social Insurance and Allied Services.* New York: Macmillan, 1942.

Boston, J., P. Dalziel and S. St. John (eds.). *Redesigning New Zealand's Welfare State.* Auckland: Oxford University Press, 1998.

Brittan, Samuel. *Capitalism with a Human Face.* London: Edward Elgar, 1995.

Campbell, B., M. T. Gutierrez Haces, A. Jackson, M. Larudee. *Pulling Apart: The Deterioration of Employment and Income in North America under Free Trade.* Ottawa: Canadian Centre for Policy Alternatives, 1999.

Canada. *Improving Social Security in Canada—Guaranteed Income: A*

Supplementary Paper. Cat. No. MP90-2/15-1995. Ottawa: Minister of Supply and Services, 1995.

Canada. *Poverty in Canada:* Report of the Special Senate Committee on Poverty. Ottawa: Minister of Supply and Services Canada, 1971; rpt. 1976.

Canada. *Royal Commission on the Economic Union and the Development Prospects for Canada.* Toronto: University of Toronto Press, 1985. In particular: vol. 2, part 5, chap. 19, The Income Security System.

Canadian Centre for Policy Alternatives and Choices: A Coalition for Social Justice. *Alternative Federal Budget Papers 1998.* Ottawa: CCPA, 1998.

Canadian Council on Social Development. *Guaranteed Annaul Income: An Integrated Approach. Ottawa: The Runge Press, 1973.*

Chancer, L. "Benefitting from Pragmatic Vision, Part I: The Case for Guaranteed Income in Principle." In S. Aronowitz and J. Cutler (eds.), *Post-Work: The Wages of Cybernation.* New York: Routledge, 1998.

Clark, C., and J. Healy. *Pathways to a Basic Income.* Dublin: CORI 1997.

Cordell, A., and T. R. Ide. *The New Wealth of Nations.* Toronto: Between the Lines, 1997.

Cudmore, James. "Study Paints Bleak Job Scene in Canada." *The National Post* June 3, 1999.

Daly, H., and J. Cobb. *For the Common Good.* Boston: Beacon Press, 1989.

Deutsch, J. "Mackintosh on the Economic Background of Federal-Provincial Relations." *Papers Presented at the Mackintosh Symposium on the Occasion of the Opening of Mackintosh-Corry Hall.* Mimeo. Kingston: Queen's University, October 18, 1974.

Dobell, R. "The 'Dance of the Deficit' and the Real World of Wealth: Re-thinking Economic Management for Social Purpose." In *Family Security in Insecure Times, Vol. 2: Perspectives,* 197-226. Ottawa: Canadian Council on Social Development, 1996.

Dominguez, J., and V. Robin. *Your Money or Your Life.* New York: Penguin Books, 1992.

Duffy, A., D. Glenday and N. Pupo (eds.). *Good Jobs, Bad Jobs, No Jobs: The Transformation of Work in the 21st Century.* Toronto: Harcourt Brace, 1997.

Freeman, C., and L. Soete. *Work for All or Mass Unemployment: Computerised Technical Change into the 21st Century.* London: Pinter, 1994.

Garraty, J. *Unemployment in History: Economic Thought and Public Policy.* New York: Harper & Row. 1978.

Gorz, A. *Misères du present, richess du possible.* Paris: Galilee, 1997.

_____ *Paths to Paradise: On the Liberation from Work.* London: Pluto Press, 1985.

Grady, P., R. Howse, and J. Maxwell. *Redefining Social Security.* Kingston: Queen's University, School of Policy Studies, 1995.

Graham, George. *Financial Times.* London, May 17, 1999.

Greider, W. *One World, Ready or Not.* New York, Simon and Schuster, 1997.

Guest, D. *The Emergence of Social Security in Canada.* Vancouver: University of British Columbia Press, 1997.

Haq, M., ul-, I. Kaul and I. Grunberg (eds.). *The Tobin Tax: Coping with Financial Volatility.* New York: Oxford University Press, 1996.

Healy, S., and B. Reynolds. *Surfing the Income Net.* Dublin: Justice Commission, Conference of Religious of Ireland, 1998.

Hirst, P., and G. F. Thompson. *Globalization in Question: The International Economy and the Possibilities of Governance.* Cambridge, UK: Polity Press, 1996.

Hum, D. *Federalism and the Poor: A Review of the Canada Assistance Plan.* Toronto: Ontario Economic Council, 1983.

————. "UISP and the Macdonald Commisssion: Reform and Restraint." *Canadian Public Policy,* XII: supplement, 1986.

————, and W. Simpson. *Income Maintenance Work Effort and the Canadian Mincome Experiment.* Ottawa: Minister of Supply and Services Canada, 1991.

Huws, U. *Flexibility and Security.* Citizen's Income Trust Paper No. 3. London, UK: Citizen's Income Trust, 1997.

Kesselman, J. R. "The Royal Commission's Proposals for Income Security Reform." *Canadian Public Policy* XII: supplement, February 1986.

Jordan, Bill. *The New Politics of Welfare.* London: Sage, 1998.

Kitchen, B. *A Guaranteed Income: A New Look at an Old Idea.* Toronto: Social Planning Council of Metropolitan Toronto, 1986.

Korten, D. *When Corporations Rule the World.* West Hartford, CN.: Kumarian Press and San Francisco: Berrett-Koehler, 1995.

Lerner, S. "The Future of Work in North America: Good Jobs, Bad Jobs, Beyond Jobs" *Futures* 26/2: 185-96, March 1994.

————. "How Will North America Work in the Twenty-first Century?" In J. Davis, T. Hirschl and M. Stack (eds.). *Cutting Edge.* London: Verso, 1997.

Lipietz, A. *Towards a New Economic Order: Postfordism, Ecology and Democracy.* Oxford, UK: Oxford University Press, 1992.

Marsh L. *Report on Social Security for Canada.* Toronto: University of Toronto Press, 1975, first published: Ottawa: King's Printer, 1943.

McCracken, M. "Introduction." In Arthur Cordell and T. Ran Ide with L. Soete and K. Kamp, *The New Wealth of Nations.* Toronto: Between the Lines, 1997, 12.

McQuaig, L. *Shooting the Hippo.* Toronto: Penguin Books, 1995.

————. *The Cult of Impotence.* Toronto: Viking, 1998.

————. *The Wealthy Banker's Wife.* Toronto: Penguin Books, 1993.

Needham, R. "Understanding the Canadian Economy—III—The Capitalist Development of Canada." Waterloo: University of Waterloo, 1997.

OECD. *Societal Cohesion and the Globalizing Economy.* Paris: OECD, 1997.

Offe, C. "Full Employment: Asking the Wrong Question?" In E. Eriksen and J. Loftager (eds.). *The Rationality of the Welfare State.* Oslo: Scandinavian University Press, 1996.

Polanyi, K. *The Great Transformation: The Political and Economic Origins of Our Times.* Boston: Beacon Press, 1957, originally published 1944.

Pollin, R., and S. Luce. *The Living Wage: Building a Fair Economy.* New York: The New Press, 1998.

Reich, R. *The Work of Nations: Preparing Ourselves for the 21st Century.* New York: Knopf, 1992.

Reid, A. *Shakedown: How the New Economy Is Changing Our Lives.* Toronto: Doubleday Canada, 1996.

Reynolds, B., and S. Healy. *Towards an Adequate Income for All.* Dublin: CORI, 1994.

————. *An Adequate Income Guarantee.* Dublin: CORI, 1995.

————. *Progress, Values and Public Policy.* Dublin: CORI, 1996.

Rifkin, J. *The End of Work.* New York: G. P. Putnam's Sons, 1995.

Simai, M. (ed.). *Global Employment: An International Investigation into the Future of Work.* Vol. 1. London: Zed Books and Tokyo: United Nations University Press, 1995.

Smiley, D. (ed.). *The Rowell-Sirois Report.* 1937 Report of the Royal Commission on Dominion-Provincial Relations. Toronto: McClelland and Stewart, 1963.

Solow, R. *Work and Welfare.* A. Gutmann (ed.). Princeton, NJ: Princeton University Press, 1998.

Stewart, W. *Dismantling the State.* Toronto: Stoddart Publishing, 1998.

Swift, J. *Wheel of Fortune: Work and Life in the Age of Falling Expectations.* Toronto: Between the Lines, 1995.

Taylor, K. S. "The Brief Reign of the Knowledge Worker: Information Technology and Technological Unemployment." Paper presented at the International Conference on the Social Impact of Information Technologies, St. Louis, MO, Oct. 12-14, 1998. http://online.bcc.ctc.edu/econ/kst/BriefReign/BRwebversion.htm.

Torjman, S., and K. Battle. *Good Work: Getting It and Keeping It.* Ottawa: Caledon Institute of Social Policy, 1999.

United Nations. *Universal Declaration of Human Rights,* 1948. http://arts.waterloo.ca/ECON/needhdata/undeclar.html.

Van Parijs, P. *Arguing for Basic Income: Ethical Foundations for a Radical Reform.* London: Verso Press, 1992.

Walter, T. *Basic Income: Freedom from Poverty, Freedom to Work.* London: Marion Boyars, 1989.

Widerquist, K. "Reciprocity and the Guaranteed Income," working paper. Annandale-on-Hudson, NY: Jerome Levy Economics Institute of Bard College, 1998. Widerquist@levy.org.

Willard, J. W. "Canadian Welfare Programmes." *Encyclopedia of Social Work.* New York: National Association of Social Workers, 1965.

Wolfson, M. "A Guaranteed Income." *Policy Options* (January 1986): 36.

Wolman, W., and A. Colamosca. *The Judas Economy.* New York: Addison-Wesley, 1997.

Yalnizyan, A. *The Growing Gap.* Toronto: Center for Social Justice, 1998.

Yalnizyan, A., T. R. Ide, and A. Cordell. *Shifting Time.* Toronto: Between the Lines, 1994.

CONTRIBUTORS

Sally Lerner is currently an adjunct associate professor in the Department of Environment and Resource Studies at the University of Waterloo. She was a founding member of the department in 1970 and served as its chair from 1994 to 1996, when she took early retirement. In October 1993, she convened the Futurework Group to analyze and foster public discussion of the social, economic, political and educational implications of the changing nature of work. She initiated the "Futurework" list on the Internet in December 1994. She is currently a member of the Leadership Round Table for OP2000, a poverty-reduction project in the Region of Waterloo.

Charles M. A. Clark is professor of Economics at St. John's University, New York. His past positions include visiting professor, University College, Cork, Ireland. Prof. Clark earned his Ph.D. at the New School for Social Research, writing his thesis under the supervision of Robert Heilbroner. He is the author of *Economic Theory and Natural Philosophy* (1992) and (with John Healy) *Pathways to a Basic Income* (1997), and editor of *History and Historians of Political Economy* (1994), *Institutional Economics and the Theory of Social Value* (1995), and (with Catherine Kavanagh) *Unemployment in Ireland* (1998).

Robert Needham, a political economist, has been at the University of Waterloo since 1965. He has held administrative positions in the Department of Economics and was a four-term president of the Faculty Association. Since 1992, he has been director of the Canadian Studies Program and has been active on the joint UW/WLU Native Studies Development Committee. His publications include *Understanding the Canadian Economy—A Political Economy Approach* (1989).

118

Dr. David C. Korten has over thirty-five years of experience in preeminent business, academic and international development institutions as well as in contemporary citizen action organizations. He is co-founder and president of the People-Centered Development Forum.

Kit Sims Taylor teaches economics—mostly online—at Bellevue Community College in Bellevue, Washington. Mr Taylor recently developed a new course on the economics of emerging technologies, which was offered (online) in the winter quarter of 1999. Email address: kitaylor@bcc.ctc.edu

Rod Dobell holds a Ph.D. in Economics from MIT and is the Francis G. Winspear Professor of Social Policy at the University of Victoria (B.C.). He has also taught at Harvard University and the University of Toronto. He served in the government of Canada as a senior advisor in the Department of Finance and as Deputy Secretary (Planning) in the Treasury Board Secretariat. He also served for two years as Director of the General Economics Branch of the Organization for Economic Co-operation and Development (OECD).

James Robertson, who has been called "that most subversive of men, the eminently reasonable revolutionary," has worked since 1973 as an independent writer, speaker and adviser. Early in his career he served in the British Cabinet Office and, subsequently, after some years' experience in systems analysis and management consulting, he set up the Inter-Bank Research Organization and directed it for the British banks. He has published a number of books, including *Beyond the Dependency Culture* and a 70-page *Briefing on Transforming Economic Life: A Millennium Challenge* (1998).

Guy Standing is senior researcher and policy analyst with the ILO. Views expressed should not be attributed to the ILO and are those of the author only.

PERMISSIONS FOR ADDITIONAL READINGS

David Korten: from *The Post-Corporate World,* pp. 168-70 and endnotes 8-13, p. 293. Reprinted with permission of the publisher. From *The Post-Corporate World,* © 1999 by David C. Korten, Berrett-Koehler Publishers, San Francisco, CA, and Kumarian Press, West Hartford, CT. All rights reserved. 1-800-929-2929.

Kit Sims Taylor: from "The Brief Reign of the Knowledge Worker," pp. 7-8, 10-13, 17-18. Reprinted with permission of the author, Kit Sims Taylor. From "The Brief Reign of the Knowledge Worker: Information Technology and Technological Unemployment." Presented at the International Conference on the Social Impact of Information Technologies, St. Louis, Missouri, October 12-14, 1998. Full copy available at http://online.bcc.ctc.edu/econ/kst/BriefReign/BRwebversion.htm

Rod Dobell: "The Dance of the Deficit and Real World of Wealth." Reprinted with permission of the publisher. From *Family Security in Insecure Times, Vol. II: Perspectives,* © 1996 by the Canadian Council on Social Development.

James Robertson: "Resource Taxes and Green Dividends: A Combined Package." Reprinted with permission of the author, James Robertson. This paper was presented at a Conference on "Sharing Our Common Heritage," held in Oxford (UK) on May 14, 1998. Copies of the conference proceedings are available from the Adminstrator, the Oxford Centre for the Environment, Ethics and Society (OCEES), Mansfield College, University of Oxford OX1 3TF.

Guy Standing: from "Seeking Equality of Security in the Era of Globalisation," pp. 4-9. Reprinted with permission of the author, Guy Standing. This excerpt is taken from a speech given to Brazilian trade unionists in 1998. The theme was elaborated in Guy Standing, *Global Labour Flexibility: Seeking Distributive Justice* (Basingstoke and New York: Macmillan and St. Martin's Press, 1999).